| DATE DUE | | | |
|---|---|---|---|
| | | | |
| | | | |
| | | | |
| | | | |
| | | | |
| | | | |
| | | | |
| | | | |
| | | | |
| | | | |
| | | | |
| | | | |

# The
# Interests of
# Criticism

*An Introduction to Literary Theory*

**HAZARD ADAMS**
University of California, Irvine

 HARCOURT, BRACE & WORLD, INC.

New York     Chicago     San Francisco     Atlanta

Acknowledgments

The Clarendon Press, Oxford: for permission to reprint excerpts from *The Dialogues of Plato*, (1953), translated by Benjamin Jowett.

New Directions Publishing Corporation and MacGibbon & Kee Ltd: for permission to reprint "The Red Wheelbarrow" by William Carlos Williams from his *Collected Earlier Poems*. Copyright 1938 by William Carlos Williams.

The University of Chicago Press: for permission to reprint excerpts from "Literary Criticism and the Concept of Imitation in Antiquity" by Richard McKeon and from "William Empson, Contemporary Criticism, and Poetic Diction" by Elder Olson. Both of these appeared in *Critics and Criticism* edited by R. S. Crane, copyright 1952.

To My Colleagues in The University of California, Irvine, during its first year, 1965–66.

# PREFACE

The aim of this book is to introduce the prospective student of literature to the fundamental problems of critical theory by showing him how the basic questions have been stated and answered by critics present and past. It is not meant to provide a syllabus for a course in critical theory, but rather to present a variety of basic issues upon which further discussion can be built. It requires little or no previous knowledge of criticism or theory and enables the student to approach any discussion of literature on a more rewarding level of sophistication.

No book of this sort can or should be written without the author's having taken his own position, if only through his choice of issues for discussion. I have tried not to be obnoxiously opinionated, but I have not avoided following my own inclinations. Teachers and students will, I hope, enjoy quarreling with me. Literary theory is no place for someone who does not like a good argument. Let it, however, be carried on without malice and in high good humor toward a common end—the greater understanding and appreciation of literary art.

Hazard Adams

# CONTENTS

The Interests of Criticism:
An Introduction to Literary Theory

# 1 THE GROUND OF CRITICAL INQUIRY

The question fundamental to literary study is, What is literature? Unfortunately it is an ambiguous question. It may mean, What things will we call literature? Or it may mean, Assuming we know what objects we are talking about, how are we to define the word? in terms of what these objects do, how they are made, or what they resemble? No matter how we interpret it, the question is an immensely difficult one. This book will not succeed in answering it; I know of no book that does.

Nevertheless, the question is worth asking, indeed very important to ask. If we speculate freely about it, we shall discover many things in the process. including some reasons why an answer is not likely. Perhaps as we proceed, we shall discover that some routes of speculation carry us further than others and that some answers simply will not do. This knowledge alone, it seems to me, will be a considerable advance.

To ignore the question is, I think, a disservice to literature, to ourselves, and to the task of building a better culture. Every serious student of literature is in varying degrees a builder or vivifier of the culture. It behooves each one to know what he is talking about. He must understand the relation of literature to the life around him, and this is a complex matter. In a period during which the scientist seems, in the public eye, so certain a source of wisdom, it is all the more important for the student of literature to know what the artist is about and to formulate clearly to himself the functions of literature and its nature.

To study properly the question I have proposed, one must go back to fundamental philosophical questions and exercise the patience of disciplined thought. The problem of the relation of literature to culture is first a problem of definitions. It involves a long search through a large body of philosophical material, working finally toward some formulations of principles that can be carried into the realm of our actual reading and judgment of literary works. This book cannot promise to reach all the way toward those principles or toward demonstration of critical methodologies (it may even deny that methodology is possible). Its aim is more modest. It seeks to provide a discussion of a number of fundamental problems of literary theory. It suggests that the student of literature should ask certain questions, be aware of what questions have been asked before, and understand the answers proposed in the past; for inquiry into the nature of literature has a history from which much can be learned. Even when literary theory has wandered in circles or down blind alleys (and it often has) it has failed in ways that deserve our contemplation. If we think otherwise and ignore that history, we tend to make the same false turns and find ourselves less able to understand why certain problems exist in the forms in which they have been bequeathed to us. Literary theory advances often by negation, by the sloughing away of inadequate ideas, by the attempt to sharpen distinctions. Indeed, the history of literary theory has been mainly a series of struggles out of positions recognized, almost as soon as attained, as philosophically untenable. Some of these positions are still held, albeit unconsciously, by large numbers of people embarking on formal literary study. Often in the normal course of events, these positions are not subjected to searching criticism. This book begins by bringing the history of thought about literature to bear upon the subject's present condition. I hope the reader finds what it has to say sufficient reason to examine his own assumptions.

The following words of R. P. Blackmur (1904–65) make a useful beginning, providing a general statement and an acceptable puzzle: "Literature," he observes, "is the bearer (the vehicle but implicated) of all the modes of understanding of which *words* are capable, and not only that: it also bears, sets in motion or life, certain modes which words merely initiate and symbolize." [1] Perhaps this is too mysterious; perhaps a book is required to explain exactly what definition is meant here. If the reader returns to this quotation from time to time through the book, he

[1] R. P. Blackmur, "Notes on Four Categories in Criticism" in *The Lion and the Honeycomb* (New York: Harcourt, Brace & World, 1955), p. 213.

should be able to test either the book's capacity to teach or his to learn or both.

Let us begin again: The question whether there is any such thing as literature or whether the word "literature" is simply another example of what Wittgenstein called the "bewitchment of language" is both fundamental and embarrassing. Do all the things we call literature have anything in common besides words? Perhaps the question is embarrassing because we are asking it too soon.[2] For the moment let us assume that "literature" is a meaningful term, that there are ways of using literature and ways of making it. Let us also admit provisionally the possibility of synthetic theories that emphasize literature as a whole, theories that emphasize the heterogeneity of literary objects, and theories that deny the possibility of any synthetic theory. It will appear, I think, from our examination of the range of criticism that both synthetic and heterogeneous drives are necessary to literary theory and dependent on each other, like Gog and Magog, Yin and Yang.

Usually the sorts of speculation we are talking about go under the name "criticism," but the term has other meanings that may complicate our attempts to discuss it in an orderly way. Basically, criticism is a branch of philosophy related to aesthetics, when that word is broadly defined. But criticism also commonly refers to other activities—to interpretive analysis of literary works, to disciplined inquiry into evaluation, and, on another level, to any issuance of judgment upon a literary work. The latter includes, of course, book-reviewing as it occurs everywhere, from the little magazines and literary journals to the daily newspapers and women's clubs. It even includes, I suppose, the judgments of those who say they do not know anything about art but know what they like.

We are concerned here with criticism as an inquiry into the nature and function of literature, because to be so concerned is to face fundamental questions prior to or at least intertwined with the problem of value. Establishment of the value of something is intertwined with what we think it is or does.

In the history of criticism, literature has been thought to be many things and to do many things, perhaps because there have

[2] In raising the question, I do not have in mind the view, current in some quarters, that "contemporary literature" is a contradiction in terms and that a literature cannot be said really to exist until the perpetrators of it are safely dead, the proper bibliographies issued, and every printing error tracked down.

been numerous vantages established from which to view it, each of which presents its own insights and limitations. The four chapters immediately following this one give their attention to various important vantages from which literature has been observed, to the compatibility or opposition of these vantages, and to their historical development. The aim of these chapters is to demonstrate how certain intellectual predicaments arose and have remained to perplex us.

Two poles between which such an inquiry may work both historically and theoretically are the idea of literature as *mimesis* and the idea of literature as *poiesis*. These terms serve to emphasize two views of the literary work and of the poet and his activity. In short (for this is the subject of Chapter 2), as far back as and even before Plato, the literary work has been considered an imitation, a copy, or a representation of something. On the other hand, it has also been considered an object made, created, a "poem" in the ancient Greek sense of the word.[3] These two views have sometimes appeared to be compatible, sometimes contradictory. They are occasioned by different vantages, dependent in turn on what imitation and creation have meant at various times; our most vexing problem is that our terms have so often shifted their meanings.

Introduction of the word *mimesis* raises the question of what is being imitated. Over the centuries those who have insisted that literature does imitate have been in disagreement over the object of imitation or over what imitation itself implies. At the same time, there has been a strong tradition that views poems as fundamentally creations or inventions, and it has included views ranging from outright rejection of imitation to doctrines that insist that poems improve on what they copy or that, indeed, we have had it all backwards: Nature copies art.[4]

The first literary theorist of record was very uneasy about both the mimetic and creative functions of poetry. Plato obviously admired the powers of the literary artist and was, in fact, an artist of considerable powers himself, but he did not trust those powers. He attacked the poet for imitating reality as we experience it and thus working at two removes from the ultimate reality of the Platonic forms, or ideas. He distrusted the creative

---

[3] Throughout this book I use the word "poem" to refer to any work of literary art and "poet" to refer to its maker.

[4] This strange assertion, as we shall see, is not as outrageous as it appears, once we know what it means. The case for it is cleverly made in Oscar Wilde's essay "The Decay of Lying" (1889).

powers of the poet because they seemed to escape the reign of rationality, endangering the search for ultimate truth. Yet Plato was apparently pained to make his indictment. In the *Republic,* Plato's Socrates would deport any poets who might happen upon his commonwealth but only after anointing them with myrrh and setting garlands upon their heads, perhaps because he could not finally be sure that the poets did not have the gods on their side.

Aristotle rescued the idea of imitation from Plato's attack. Several interpreters have held that Aristotle was answering Plato; others have argued that in redefining the term *mimesis* he was making an independent assertion. In either case there is no doubt that with Aristotle the word's meaning shifted. Over the long stretch of history since he wrote his *Poetics* the term *mimesis* has exhibited more lives than the cat, and since rediscovery of the *Poetics* in the Renaissance it has taken more shapes than Proteus. Usually imitative theories emphasize the relation of the poem to something external to it—reality, the world, nature. The history of imitation is a tangled one because of the variety of objects considered possible of imitation and (to look at the problem in another way) the shifting meanings given to words supposedly referring to such objects. Thus we have Plato arguing that the poet imitates imitations of the Platonic ideas, Aristotle arguing that tragedy imitates an action, and eighteenth-century critics locating the objects of imitation in abstract ideas or general nature. Partly because of the idea that poetry imitates, the history of literary theory has gone hand in hand with the history of philosophy, particularly the history of epistemology. Most imitative theories imply that poems tell us something about the world. How we know about the world or whatever it is we do know is a question in epistemology.

It is clear, of course, that poets make something more than or even other than servile copies of nature or of anything else. Aristotle himself emphasized the formal structure of literary art, and many commentators insist that for him imitation did not mean copying at all. Philip Sidney (1554–86), influenced by both Plato and Aristotle, put very gracefully the notion that the poet grows another nature and a better one, "freely ranging within the zodiac of his own wit." With the crisis in epistemology traceable from Descartes through Locke, Berkeley, and Hume to Kant, the emphasis in criticism swung from imitation to creation. For Samuel Taylor Coleridge (1772–1834), a critic deeply schooled in the philosophical speculations of his time, the imagination partly, at least, makes reality; and the poet's act, a product of what Coleridge calls "the secondary imagination," becomes an act of creation on the analogy of God's creativity:

> The primary Imagination I hold to be the living power and prime Agent of all human Perception, and as a repetition in the finite mind of the eternal act of creation in the infinite *I am.* The secondary Imagination I consider as an echo of the former . . .[5]

As an analogy of God's "eternal act," what the poet does is also an imitation of sorts, though perhaps not a conscious one. The imitation, however, is of God's *process* of original creation rather than of objects. There is ground to think that Aristotle, too, may have been talking about imitation in art as imitating the *way* and not *what* nature creates. In this case Coleridge would seem to be Aristotelian but with a different idea of deity.

After Kant and Coleridge, the idea of the independent integrity of the literary work gained strength from the movements known as *Symbolisme* and *Art pour l'art,* from the New Criticism of the nineteen-thirties and forties, and from neo-Kantian philosophers of symbolic form. Ernst Cassirer (1874–1945), one of the foremost of the last group, insisted that art creates its own "universe of discourse"; a system of symbols makes a reality for us by organizing the undifferentiated flux of experience that otherwise is devoid of meaning and therefore in a sense unreal. We shall return to these matters in Chapter 2.

Aristotle's *Poetics* established the ground for most subsequent imitative theories, no matter how un-Aristotelian they turned out to be. It also led to considerations of the affective quality of tragedy through its famous remark that tragedy brings about a catharsis of pity and fear. An overwhelming number of interpreters of Aristotle have assumed that the remark refers to the reaction of the audience of the tragedy. Recently, however, certain interpreters have suggested that it describes what happens to the characters in the play or how the play moves structurally toward its proper artistic conclusion. In any case, even before Alexander Gottlieb Baumgarten (1712–62) invented the word "aesthetics" in the eighteenth century, there had been plenty of consideration of what a literary work should do to its readers and what, in reality, it does do. Is its purpose primarily to delight? To teach? If it simply imitates, does the imitation impart knowledge? Finally, can literature be defined or judged

---

[5] From the famous thirteenth chapter of the *Biographia Literaria.*

primarily in terms of its effect? Perhaps wisely, Aristotle did not make his definition depend on an empirical test of audience reaction; instead he saw pleasure as a product of poetic excellence, not an external standard by which to define or judge the work.

Plato grounded his objection to poetry partly on the nefarious effect that it could work on the populace. Aristotelians generally have seen tragedy as performing upon the audience a catharsis and therefore having a beneficial effect. There has long been a tradition that emphasizes literature as entertaining or didactic or both. In its didactic function literary art may be thought to provide knowledge or moral exhortation. By the same token, some literature may be thought to impart false knowledge or immorality. On the other hand, critics and poets threatened with censorship have often felt themselves compelled to issue proclamations that literature gives no knowledge, that it is neither moral nor immoral, that the reader is of no importance, that poets write only to the Muse, and so forth. In recent times sophisticated psychological theories have given rise to ideas asserting the psychological worth of literature to the reader. In spite of this activity, and sometimes because of it, the relation between literature and the reader remains a fascinating and murky one. Perhaps it always will be murky, and perhaps this is even a good thing. Chapter 3 considers some of these problems.

When Coleridge saw the imaginative act, a copy of God's creative act, as the essence of art, he was emphasizing an aspect of criticism nearly untouched by Aristotle but of the greatest interest to critics of the Romantic age. This was the relation of the poet to what he makes. When William Wordsworth (1770–1850) defended his own poetic practice in his preface to the second edition of *Lyrical Ballads,* he discovered himself describing what kind of man a poet must be. When Coleridge attempted to define "poem" in the *Biographia Literaria,* he too was driven first to define "poet." When John Keats (1795–1821) considered Shakespeare's plays, he was impelled to consider the quality of Shakespeare's mind. For many of the Romantics it was less important that the poet reflect the world than that he express himself. One reason for this was that with the development of philosophical idealism the creative powers of the mind were thought to take precedence over the mind's imitative or representational powers. Reality was now partly constructed by the mind, and therefore to imitate reality was to express the mind. Furthermore, the mind was now seen as more than rational, or, rather, irrationality was valued because it included virtuous sentiments. A poem became, in the famous phrase of Wordsworth, a "spontaneous overflow of powerful feelings."

Under the domination of these interests, literary study turned to literary biography and then to psychological analysis of the man behind the poem. A direction that critical theory has at times taken—from poem to author—is the subject of Chapter 4. But in the latter part of the nineteenth century there was a reaction. A famous twentieth-century poem by Archibald Mac-Leish asserts: "A poem should not mean but be." The statement that a poem should "be" has a surface meaning we shall all probably accept without question. A poem can be considered on the analogy of a statue, which has an independent existence—matter transformed into a specific shape. We can treat it as an object, walking around it, so to speak, viewing it from various angles. There it is. But poems have words, and words have meanings. What is meant by "A poem should not mean"? [6] Clearly the problem of what meaning is presents itself here. Criticism must be concerned with it.

In brief, it has recently been held that literature is a mode of discourse that operates according to principles different from those of logical discourse and that since meaning is usually defined in terms of logical discourse it is not applicable to literature. Subsequent questions concern themselves with the nature of literary discourse and just how it does differ from other modes. In other words, the attempt is to define for literature what the line from MacLeish's poem means by "be," if it is allowed to mean anything by it. This problem is at the center of contemporary critical speculation, and Chapter 5 is devoted to its consideration.

Chapters 2 through 5 form a unit that approaches its subject historically as well as speculatively, a grasp of the history of the subject being indispensable to the reader's understanding of each problem's many curious difficulties. The problems are not, of course, really separable, but related to each other. Thus it is required that some backtracking take place now and then. Two fundamental ideas inform the discussion. One is that literary theory marches with epistemology. The other is that a fundamental question to ask about any critical pronouncement is, Where

[6] Or, because these words are from a poem, MacLeish's "Ars Poetica," are we to assume our question is improper and the statement does not mean anything? Resolution of this dilemma is one concern of this book and criticism generally.

does it locate the poem? In nature (or as a copy of it), in its "message," in the reader, in the poet, or strictly, in its own words or structures?

No matter where it finally does locate the poem, a critical theory emphasizes one of two fundamental aims or both: description and evaluation. Naturally, most theories mix these, since all evaluation supposes some description and description can imply judgment, if only that the object has been worth describing or naming as literature. Just as some theorists describe literature generally, so others interest themselves in particular works. Just as some theorists seek to establish the value of literature as a cultural form, so others evaluate single literary objects. Chapter 6 considers how recent critical theorists have dealt with the problems bequeathed to them, seeking new vantages from which they can either separate description and evaluation or try to keep them together.

The history of evaluation has taken many turns. In Plato we find an influential negative evaluation of literature as a whole but not much useful description. Aristotle, following the method he had employed in his other systematic treatises, provided in the *Poetics* the earliest known descriptive criticism. Interpreters of other sorts have since abounded: Biblical typologists, allegorical interpreters of Greek myth, medieval allegorists, the practitioners of *explication de texte* who abound today in many schools, psychoanalytical interpreters representing various persuasions, and anthropological critics interested in myth and ritual as literary patterns. It is perhaps a paradox of literary history that as literature has come to insist that it does not "mean," critics have developed more and more complex ways of finding meaning in it.

Since the ancients, evaluation of literature as a whole has been made from every conceivable point of view. Aristotelians, if not Aristotle, emphasized the value to the audience of tragedy's catharsis, and presumably Aristotle would have found other values in other genres. Longinus emphasized literature's possible sublimity. Renaissance critics emphasized moral value and delight; Romantic critics, its expressive power and sincerity. Single literary works have been subjected to a variety of modes of judgment from Matthew Arnold's touchstones to broad monolithic standards of irony, ambiguity, and formal complexity such as we find in the New Criticism. This movement, which developed in America in the nineteen-thirties and dominated critical theory for two decades, was associated with the tradition of *explication de texte,* stressing description of formal structures and techniques rather than allegorization as part of a process working toward evaluation. In theory, at least, "meaning," or rather "being," was sought through examination of technique. Blackmur wrote: "If the dominant ideas of a work may have a technical function, cannot we also ask, are not the technical resources and limits of literature sometimes the *object,* even the virtual truth, of the work—so far as the work is susceptible to discourse?" [7] The New Criticism's emphasis on evaluation was twofold. It sought to discriminate among works, but, possibly more important in the long run, it also made a defense of literature as a cultural form. Critics of the fifties and sixties have continued to be concerned with this matter, several following along in a Kantian way, others reconstituting criticism according to Aristotelian categories, and still others seeking theoretical sanction in phenomenology. Through all this the exact function of the critic is surreptitiously being reassessed.

Most of the criticism mentioned thus far has been of the systematic sort or at least has been treated as of interest because of the possibility of its contributing to an orderly approach to the question of the nature of literature and literary value. It is important to balance this discussion with an acknowledgment of the importance of a kind of criticism antithetical in most ways to systematic theory. In the final chapter, therefore, there is a rough division of critics into two classes, the "systematic" and the "violent," followed by a discussion of "violent" criticism.[8] Critics are particularly classifiable in this way according to their roles as evaluators. The violent critic is usually a member of some literary movement, the principles of which he wishes to defend. His polemics are part of literary politics. Among those of this century Ezra Pound, Robert Graves, and D. H. Lawrence are good examples. These critics usually support the kind of literature they like or write, without much respect for philosophical consistency and even less respect for their forebears. Systematic critics, often academic scholars, tend to formulate principles of description and evaluation that claim some degree of universality and historical perspective.

[7] Blackmur, *op. cit.,* p. 214.
[8] My term "violent" may be itself too violent, but a word like "polemical" will not quite do, since there have been plenty of polemics among systematic theorists. There has even been violent polemic. The term "impressionistic" will not do either, for there is a theoretical ground—an epistemological one —for the impressionist. Perhaps there is *no* adequate word for the sort of critic I am going to describe.

These two impulses in criticism are at odds. The violent critic, intent on his end, seeking to justify his kind of art, is impatient with the systematic critic, whom he often accuses (sometimes with good reason) of academic stodginess and failure to appreciate the contemporary. The systematic critic can usually counter by saying that the violent critic is irrational and egocentric in his defense and excessively exclusive in his judgments. Once the systematic critic catches up with what the violent critic is defending, he devises a system to devour it, forcing the violent critic into agreement with the establishment. The violent critic's advantage, on the other hand, is that since he is often a poet himself, his own violent criticism—no matter how wrongheaded—is of continuing interest for the light it throws on his own art. The systematic critic and the violent critic are antagonists, but they require each other, and literary theory requires both.

If we can become Olympian enough, far above polemics and systems, perhaps we can begin to see that criticism changes and develops dialectically. Like all speculative ventures, there is no end to it. The critic tries to make a theory, but if his mind is open, even as he tries he knows that it will be imperfect, that it will be superseded, that eventually his efforts will take on something of the aspect of an historical curiosity. Literature is to the critic as nature is to the scientist: it keeps secrets from us all. The critic wrestles with literature as with Proteus.

But this is not ground for despair or for rejection of critical activity. Criticism must continue as a responsible activity, for people will continue to make irresponsible critical judgments and irresponsibly define the nature and function of literature. Enough of this goes on every day to make those of us who think art important barely suppress a savage rage. In order to remain responsible, critical theory must continually make a critique of itself, act against its own excesses and timidities. Criticism can never be final. The human condition and the limitations of language prevent it from ever reaching completion. But it had better not be stillborn or infantile. That would be disastrous for art and ultimately for civilization.

# 2 IMITATION AND CREATION

Let me be fanciful for a moment and imagine the source of imitation theories, in their crude form at least, in some primitive man's judgment upon a friend's wood carving: "Yes, that looks very much like a bull. Congratulations." The appearance of another carving must have occasioned a comparison: "This is a better bull than that one." If asked what he meant by "better," the speaker might well have answered: "Why, this one is *more like a bull* than the other." There is cause, however, to wonder whether the answer discloses the real reasons for his preference. The criterion of accuracy is itself subject to various interpretations. Would the painstaking representation of a bull with, say, each hair on its back clearly delineated be more accurate than a general impression of a bull? Would a series of vital statistics indicating the size and shape of the average bull be truer than the impression? Would the essence of bull be preferable to a particular bull? The first artist to answer, "Well, that's the way *I* see the bull," is probably lost somewhere in prehistory.

Another interesting question is raised by the old saying, "A picture is worth a thousand words." By "picture" in this saying we usually mean a diagram or plan such as an engineer or architect might draw. For his purpose the picture *is* worth a thousand words—and more. But if we were to compare a primitive wall drawing, or any drawing, of a bull with a poem about a bull, we would not be able to enlist the old saying in the drawing's behalf. The drawing and the poem are clearly not comparable, even if they seem to imitate the same object. Nor would a butcher's diagram showing where the steaks come from be comparable to either. A diagram is always a surrogate. It has no importance beyond its relation to the object that it denotes. Plans for a house are drawn to help build the house. Is the wall drawing or the poem a surrogate for or even subordinate to the bull represented in it?

There are questions one might want to ask about the artist's intent. Did the artist make his carving because he wanted to *represent* a bull? The object might have been intended as an effigy in some religious ceremony. In that sense, perhaps it *was* the bull, as it is believed that the bread and wine are the body and blood of Jesus. To think of the object in that way is to treat it as an anthropological object. Perhaps it is possible to define it in a different way as an artistic object, an object of criticism. To define it in such a way may free it to some extent from being a surrogate or copy.

But perhaps the artist was setting out to amuse himself with wood and knife when over the slope there appeared a bull, a subject come conveniently to hand. It is clear that the terms under which we consider the object might change the judgment delivered upon it from one based on accuracy, whatever accuracy is, to one based on some other criterion:

1. "Yes, that's clearly a bull, but will the wood burn quickly, and will the gods be pleased?"
2. "You know, I can't see it as a bull particularly, but my, what an impressive shape!"
3. "Hmmm, six legs. That's interesting."
4. "Well, I certainly have learned something about you from looking at your bull!"

Remarks similar to these are made about poems today, even as they must have been in prehistoric times. As far as we know, it has always been assumed that literature is in some way related to the world, that it *represents*. The earliest remarks about literature that have survived mention imitation, or *mimesis* (μίμησις). A hymn to Apollo, as far back as the seventh century B.C., says that the hymn-singers imitate varieties of speech. The poet Pindar, in the fifth century B.C., was clearly interested in being as faithful as possible to the facts. His odes celebrated actual events. But it is important to consider that these events would be forgotten were it not for our interest in his poems. The facts he has preserved are not the important matter. True, today we would still want a Pindaric poet to be faithful to the facts, but all of his care in this matter would not suffice if he failed in other ways.

The poem is apparently not primarily defined in terms of the facts it contains.

The first surviving attack on poetry assumes that poetry imitates and that because it imitates it cannot possibly be true. Furthermore, the argument goes, poetry is dangerous, because it distracts us from the pursuit of truth. This is, of course, Plato's argument against admitting the poet to his ideal Republic. Plato makes his judgment solely on the basis of the so-called content or subject matter of poetry without respect to the medium of expression. This single-minded approach gives his argument its apparent strength but also its ultimate weakness.

The argument depends greatly upon whether or not we agree to locate truth or reality where Plato does. Plato locates it in what he calls the ideas, or forms. The idea of a bed, which exists in God, so to speak, is the only real bed. The beds of earthly bed-makers are imitations of the idea. The artist, in turn, imitates these imitations:

> Which is the art of painting designed to be—an imitation of things as they are, or as they appear—of appearance or of reality?
> Of appearance, he said.
> Then the imitator is a long way off the truth, and can reproduce all things because he lightly touches on a small part of them, and that part an image. [*Republic*][1]

By this judgment a poet's imitation is twice removed from truth and bound to be obfuscatory.

Now, if we are concerned only with the subject matter and not its form, we might possibly agree with Plato that to obtain a true representation of, say, a shoe, we should go to a shoemaker and not a poet:

> A painter will paint a cobbler, carpenter, or any other artisan, though he knows nothing of their arts; and, if he is a good painter, he may deceive children or simple persons when he shows them his picture of a carpenter from a distance, and they will fancy that they are looking at a real carpenter.
> Certainly.
> And surely, my friend, this is how we should regard all such claims: whenever any one informs us that he has found a man who knows all the arts, and all things else that anybody knows, and every single thing with a higher degree of accuracy than any other man—whoever tells us this, I think that we can only retort that he is a simple creature who seems to have been de-

[1] Quotations from Plato are from the translation by Benjamin Jowett in his *The Dialogues of Plato*, 4th ed. (Oxford, Eng.: Clarendon Press, 1953).

ceived by some wizard or imitator whom he met, and whom he thought all-knowing, because he himself was unable to analyse the nature of knowledge and ignorance and imitation. [*Republic*]

For the purposes of this discussion, two things are involved. First, there is Plato's argument that the imitation takes the mind away from ultimate truths. Second, there is the attack on the poet because he is not expert in the things he imitates.

The first argument is related to Plato's famous assertion: "There is an ancient quarrel between philosophy and poetry." Ultimate truths, in Plato's philosophy, are arrived at by rational processes, not by the irrational processes of poetry with its appeal to concrete, sensuous experience. As A. E. Taylor has written, Plato's dialectic

would treat the initial postulates of the sciences as mere starting-points to be used for the discovery of some more ultimate premises which are not "postulated," but strictly self-luminous and evident, a real "principle of everything," and when it had discovered such a principle (or principles), it would then deduce the consequences which follow; and in this movement no appeal would be made to sensible aids to the imagination . . . .[2]

In the *Ion,* Socrates convinces Ion that when he speaks as a rhapsode and critic he must be possessed by some god and acting out of divine frenzy. In the *Republic,* Plato suggests that the same is true of poets. In the society he envisions, built on Platonic rationality, this loss of control is intolerable. Since rationality and not divine madness, no matter how awe-inspiring, is the way to ultimate truths, the poet must be banned from the Republic. The excellent remedies of measuring and counting, which do away with the deceptions to which our senses are prone, may be used to counteract the poet's dissimulations.

The second argument, the attack on the poet because he is not expert in the things he copies, raises as many problems for Plato as it does for those of us who try to make sense of it. Plato can make good his accusation against the poet only as long as he finds nothing unique in what the poet has done. He holds that the whole substance of a poem is the copies it contains. The poet who introduces a bed into his poem copies the bed-maker's copy, without necessarily knowing anything about bed-making. Plato never even admits that what the poet may be copying is the idea of a poem. For Plato, the poem is not itself a thing but a

[2] A. E. Taylor, *Plato: The Man and His Work* (Cleveland: Meridian Books, 1956), pp. 291–92.

collection of copies. Cut off from being an expert in making poems, the poet can never be an expert in anything.

Plato attacks Ion the rhapsode for the same lack of expertness and on the same grounds. In his conversation with Ion, Socrates finds that Ion, not himself an expert on chariots or chariot-racing, is unqualified to judge Homer's competence to describe the activities of a charioteer. A charioteer in this case would be a better qualified critic of Homer. In this way, Socrates talks Ion into agreeing that it is not skill that enables him to speak well about Homer, for he has no expertness, but some miraculous power possessing him. The embattled Ion is driven to make a strangely provocative answer to Socrates' attack. The conversation at the crucial point goes as follows:

> And as I have selected from the Iliad and Odyssey for you passages which describe the office of the prophet and the physician and the fisherman, do you, who know Homer so much better than I do, Ion, select for me passages which relate to the rhapsode and the rhapsode's art, and which the rhapsode ought to examine and judge of better than other men.
> All passages, I should say, Socrates.

But Socrates reminds him that he has already admitted his inability to judge the parts about chariot-racing as well as the charioteer can. If he is not an expert on some of the parts, how can he be an expert on all the parts?

The argument that Plato does not allow Ion to think of and exploit is obvious. Ion never quite reaches the point of saying that the totality of the poem is distinct from the aggregate of its parts; this is the crux of the matter. Once a whole that is more than the sum of its parts is admitted as a rational object, Plato's admonition to keep to counting and measurement fails, and his whole system of logic is revealed as inadequate to a critique of poet or critic. Ion could then claim that he is an expert on poetic wholes, if not on the specific content of a poem.

It is uncertain whether or not the historical Socrates held the same views. In a passage from the *Memorabilia* of Xenophon (430–355 B.C.) it is said that Socrates had a conversation with the sculptor Parrhasius in which they agreed that the sculptor imitates but that he may combine the attributes of many models into a new whole. Parrhasius remarked that as a sculptor he could not represent the soul, but Socrates replied that the sculptor does express the feelings of the subject in bodily mood and therefore does imitate the soul. Before Plato, then (if this passage is historically accurate), the artist was thought to have a more significant role than Plato allows him in the *Republic*; he is not merely a servile copier, and he can imitate the soul. Xenophon's Socrates has a broader idea of artistic imitation than Plato's.

In some places, however, Plato himself seems to express great admiration for poets. Although he holds that a great poet must be possessed by the Muses, and therefore produces the irrational, he admires the results:

> he who, having no touch of the Muses' madness in his soul, comes to the door and thinks that he will get into the temple by the help of art—he, I say, and his poetry are not admitted; the sane man disappears and is nowhere when he enters into rivalry with the madman. [*Phaedrus*]

In frequent remarks of this sort, Plato sows the seeds of later defenses of poetry precisely on the grounds that it *is* irrational.

Finally, however, because Plato proposes a rational quest for truth, which is equated with the good, he must make his critical judgments upon isolated parts of the poem, and the content must conform to his canons of morality. Thus in the *Lesser Hippias* he seems to judge the *Iliad* and *Odyssey* on the grounds of how good or great their respective heroes are. We shall observe judgments of this sort all through history; here it suffices to say that since Plato seems not to consider the poem an object that is more than its parts, then it follows that whatever he dislikes in the poem he will judge in isolation from the whole. He will not ask whether Odysseus' character is or is not proper for the context in which it appears. For the present it is most important to consider not only what Plato thought but also what questions he may have compelled us to ask in turn. Is the content of something its only significance? Indeed, is the content separable from its container? Does it make sense to talk about container and content at all? If a poet does imitate, does he make only a servile copy?

Plato's arguments may not seem worth our while once we examine them closely. We may conclude that he has simply muddied the waters. On the other hand, arguments similar to his are raised today, often, I suspect, by people who do not know they were raised and debated in antiquity. The argument from content still forms the basis of every polemic in behalf of censorship of the arts. But what is more important, perhaps, is that the apparent simplicity of Plato's arguments drives us to formulate new assertions about the nature of the poetic object. In fact, one suspects that despite an ironic tone, Plato was serious when he invited someone to step forward and raise convincing arguments for readmitting the poet to the Republic:

> let us assure the poetry which aims at pleasure, and the art of imitation, that if she will only prove her title to exist in a well-ordered State we shall be delighted to receive her—we are very conscious of her charms; but it would not be right on that account to betray the truth. [*Republic*]

Aristotle's assertions about the nature of tragic drama have been thought by many to be the defense Plato called for in his indictment of the poet. But Plato would not have approved, for Aristotle did not confine himself to Plato's system. He overthrew the whole doctrine of ideas and in the process redefined imitation. Starting from an antithesis between pure Being (reality) and Becoming (appearance) and proposing an imitative relationship between them, Plato found little or no relationship between art, which copies appearances, and truth. Aristotle begins by rejecting the antithesis, which affects his whole attitude toward art and changes the meaning of his words. In the *Poetics* he calls tragedy an imitation, but to him the word means something quite different from what it means to Plato. In order to consider its meaning, we must take note of the emphasis Aristotle puts on all that Plato would relegate to the realm of becoming. Aristotle does not hold that the world of appearances is merely an ephemeral copy of the changeless. He sees change as a fundamental process of nature, which he thinks of as the creative force itself. Nor is nature some force manipulating change from beyond change. Nature inheres in the objects of change as their "internal principle of motion." [3] Nature is not an outer world of objects, a copy of ideas. There is no such thing as an ideal Platonic being in Aristotle's system. There is only the direction in which nature moves.

Aristotle's best known discussion of imitation occurs in his famous and controversial definition of tragedy:

> Tragedy, then, is an imitation of an action that is serious, complete, and of a certain magnitude; in language embellished with each kind of artistic ornament, the several kinds being found in separate parts of the play; in the form of action, not of

[3] The phrase is from Richard McKeon's "Literary Criticism and the Concept of Imitation in Antiquity" in R. S. Crane, ed., *Critics and Criticism* (Chicago: Univ. of Chicago Press, 1952), p. 161.

narrative; through pity and fear effecting the proper purgation of these emotions.[4]

Aristotle's definition does not mean that tragedy copies Platonic ideas, Platonic appearances, an idea in the artist's mind, or the objective world hypothesized by science. He says that tragedy imitates actions of men, and by this he apparently does not mean slavish copying of such actions. S. H. Butcher interprets Aristotle to mean that tragedy imitates the motivation from which deeds spring, the incidents and situations brought about by the human will.[5] He remarks in his commentary: "The common original, then, from which all the arts draw is human life,—its mental processes, its spiritual movements, its outward acts issuing from deeper sources; in a word, all that constitutes the inward and essential activity of the soul." [6] Butcher is only one of Aristotle's many commentators who never tire of reiterating that Aristotelian imitation is of a process rather than of some static or moving outer object. Tragedy imitates not men but actions by men. In associating imitation with action, Aristotle apparently sought to free imitation from copying or representing objects as well as from naive realism.

Yet art does appropriate forms from nature. Unlike abstract reasoning, art does try to reproduce actions as they appear to the senses. The words of tragedy do not *resemble* what they refer to; they are a medium by which actions are imitated. In plays, of course, the words spoken represent the words spoken by the characters, but imitation does not, for Aristotle, lie in the mimicry of performance or in the verbal composition *as words*. It lies in the making of plots by means of the medium. Naturally enough, the idea of imitation grew historically out of what actors and mimics do, but by imitation Aristotle refers to the composition of the total action of the play.

In his redefinition of imitation Aristotle tries to destroy the idea of the poet as a mere copier of objects and replace it with the idea of the poet as a maker. It is particularly here that modern interpreters have differed about his meaning. The idea of the poet as a maker referred originally, no doubt, to his making verses, while the idea of *mimesis* referred to his representing things in verse. But Aristotle points out that although Homer

---

[4] Quotations from Aristotle's *Poetics* are from the translation by S. H. Butcher in his *Aristotle's Theory of Poetry and Fine Art*, 4th ed. (New York: Dover, 1951). Readers would do well to compare other translations.

[5] *Ibid.*, p. 123.

[6] *Ibid.*, p. 124.

and Empedocles both composed in verse, only Homer was a true poet, because he made plots. Furthermore, if Homer had written in prose, he would still have been more of a poet than Empedocles, who did not make plots. To Aristotle, then, there is no contradiction between poet, or maker, and imitator. The two words, in fact, define each other. The poet is a maker of plots, and these plots are imitations of actions. To imitate actions is not to mirror or copy things in nature but to make something in a way that nature makes something—that is, to have imitated nature.

Aristotle goes much farther than Socrates did in his conversation with Parrhasius. The artist does not simply recombine elements separate in their nature. The creative element in art is likened to the creativity of nature. The artist takes a form from nature and reshapes it in a different matter (or medium). This medium, which the form does not inhabit in nature, is the source of each work of art's inward principle of order and consequently of its independence from slavish copying. This principle of order Aristotle identifies with plot, which is what emerges after form is subjected to the shaping force of the medium. G. F. Else, a contemporary interpreter, has taken the following view of Aristotelian plot:

> The plot is the *structure* of the play, around which the material "parts" are laid, just as the soul is the structure of a man. It is well known that in Aristotle's biology the soul—i.e., the form—is "prior" to the body; and we shall see that he thinks of the plot as prior to the poem in exactly the same way. By this I do not mean what we mean when we say that the "story" or "myth" of Oedipus was there before Sophocles wrote his drama. For Aristotle the plot precedes the poem, but it too is essentially "made" by the poet, even if he is using traditional material.[7]

R. S. Crane, to whose recent reading of Aristotle we shall return in Chapter 6, concludes that the object that the poem imitates is not some preexistent pattern of action recognizable in human life, but the structure of action that the words or matter of the poem have helped to create and then point to. In this sense the poem imitates only what it creates. This position raises, as perhaps does Else's, the question whether imitation is really a useful term or whether its popular sense is not so opposed to its Aristotelian sense that its use can only cause confusion.

We can say, I think, that Aristotle insists that the poet

[7] G. F. Else, *Aristotle's Poetics: The Argument* (Cambridge, Mass.: Harvard Univ. Press, 1957), pp. 242–43.

creates, but not out of nothing or purely from his own sensibility. To create something, for Aristotle, means to discover its ultimate form and find, as Else observes, "a true relation which already exists somehow in the scheme of things." [8] The poet makes the meaning of events by making their structure, and he does this in a medium, a matter, which is words.

Aristotle was broadening the idea of imitation for his own purposes, one of which was to attribute intellectuality and independent creativity to the artist's imitative act. The conjunction of imitated form and artistic matter, or medium, seems to make possible in Aristotle's view an improvement on nature; thus some tragedies can imitate men as better or worse than they are in real life and in so doing can make plots with more order than we find in nature. This improvement upon nature lies principally in the heightened unity, or harmony, of the work of art provided by the medium. This unity is a unity generated by and unique to the medium and not imposed upon it, though the object of imitation and the manner of imitation are deeply involved and also tend to control the kind of unity that is achieved.

Sometimes nature's designs are clouded, but the artist's better not be. Therefore, Aristotle advises, "even coincidences are most striking when they have an air of design," and he goes on to remark:

> In composing the *Odyssey* [Homer] did not include all the adventures of Odysseus—such as his wound on Mt. Parnassus, or his feigned madness at the mustering of the host—incidents between which there was no necessary or probable connexion: but he made the *Odyssey,* and likewise the *Iliad,* to centre round an action that in our sense of the word is one. As therefore, in the other imitative arts, the imitation is one when the object imitated is one, so the plot, being an imitation of an action, must imitate one action and that a whole, the structural union of the parts being such that, if one of them is displaced or removed, the whole will be disjointed and disturbed.

By the same token, the poet is less concerned with what happened than with what may happen and prefers "probable impossibilities" to "improbable possibilities." By "probable" here Aristotle doubtless means something like "having an air of design." Probability does not refer to statistical likelihood in real life but to the structural demands the work of art makes upon itself.

Elsewhere in the *Poetics* Aristotle remarks that there is a

[8] *Ibid.,* p. 320.

sense in which the artist is guilty of an error if he describes the impossible, but if he attains his artistic ends, he is justified. Aristotle clings strongly enough to the possible so that he adds: "If, however, the end might have been as well, or better, attained without violating the special rules of the poetic art, the error is not justified." But he cannot let it go at that; a famous statement follows: "not to know that a hind has no horns is a less serious matter than to paint it inartistically."

Has Aristotle begged the question here? What is to paint artistically? What is meant by harmony and design in art? Are such things separable from imitation? Aristotle has argued hard to show, in a sort of paradox, that the creative element of the artistic work is precisely the imitation. Is art most like nature and most imitative when it is clearly emancipated from copying nature? Our questions show that Aristotle has tried to release the idea of imitation from that of servile copying. Art for Aristotle does not simply reproduce nature. It is not a slave to its content.

Aristotle's *Poetics* was lost in early Christian times and in the Middle Ages, but its influence became very strong after its rediscovery by the Italians in the sixteenth century. The idea of imitation that it espoused has been a matter for debate ever since. Despite Aristotle's efforts to save "imitation" from implying that the artist is an unimaginative copier of nature, the constant tendency has been to slip back to the more naive sense of the word. As a result the whole concept has suffered attack after attack.

Renaissance theorists held both Plato and Aristotle in immense respect. By and large, they worked within the Aristotelian vocabulary, but often they were cramped by the Platonic meaning of imitation, which tended to assert itself as a part of their Platonic orientation. Struggling against Plato while still in his debt, they sought ways of emphasizing the artist's inventiveness. We see this particularly in the work of Jacopo Mazzoni (1548–98), who in his book *On the Defense of the Comedy of Dante* (1587) makes some interesting observations about what the artist does. Mazzoni recalls that in the *Sophist* Plato divides imitation into two kinds: the icastic and the phantastic. Icastic imitation represents things that really happened, while the phantastic "is exemplified in pictures made by the caprice of the artist."[9] Since the artist may imitate in both of these ways,

[9] Quotations from Mazzoni's *Della difesa della "Commedia" di Dante* are from the translation by Allan Gilbert in his *Literary Criticism: Plato to Dryden* (Detroit: Wayne State Univ. Press, 1962), pp. 358–403.

it is clear that the essential aim of art cannot be the conveyance of factual truth. Mazzoni holds that the sole aim of art is to create an image or an idol: "The imitative arts are so called not because they use imitation, for in this sense all the arts in small or great measure use some sort of imitation, but because they imitate objects that have no being or use except from imitation and in imitation."

It is clear enough that Mazzoni is trying to protect art against the old charge that it makes only a servile copy. He also is trying to distinguish art from other modes of discourse having other aims. So he argues that although poetry does often turn out to be useful and delightful, nevertheless its end is merely to imitate. But note that, somewhat in the manner of Crane, Mazzoni makes the object imitated a creation of the poetic act, denying it a prior existence. Mazzoni goes on to imply that in a sense all artistic imitation is really phantastic imitation, even when it is apparently icastic: "The verisimilitude, then, sought after by the poets is of such a nature that it is feigned by them according to their wish."

These remarks, while holding on to the idea of imitation, tend to emphasize the poet's power to feign a reality for no other purpose than to feign it. Poetry differs from, say, history in that it does not, even when it is icastic, have as its aim the conveyance of information. However, as Lodovico Castelvetro (1505–71) points out in his commentary on Aristotle (1571), this does not mean that the poet should not form the plot of his tragedy or epic from history. To do so may, in fact, challenge the inventiveness of the poet more than copying a phantasy world.

Another Italian critic, Francesco Patrizzi (1529–97), rather than working within the idea of imitation, attacks it vigorously. It seems to him that imitation can only properly mean that of the icastic sort, which leads to narrow realism. Like Aristotle, however, he concludes that poetry is not defined by whether the subject matter is copied or feigned or by the subject matter at all. The defining element is the manner in which the material is treated. Unfortunately he is vague about what a poetic treatment actually consists of.

Among the Italian critics, then, we have the work of art hanging precariously between an idea of it as a copy and a less clearly delineated but emerging concept of the work as an invention of its author. In the history of criticism we see the latter idea take progressively clearer shape as new developments occur in epistemology. The Romantic movement of the late eighteenth and early nineteenth centuries is a watershed. However, the critical movements associated with Neoclassicism, Naturalism, and Realism imply even more extreme ideas of imitation.

But before we trace these two historical threads it is well to pause briefly with the well-known English critical work by Philip Sidney. It has been said that his "Defence of Poesie" (*c.* 1583, published posthumously in 1595) lacks originality. However, if it repeats ideas current in the time, it does so with a remarkable grace and clarity that make it both useful and delightful. In spite of the derivative nature of many of his ideas, Sidney emphasizes some ideas more than others. As a result some stand out in a new way. The idea of imitation is introduced only after he asserts that the poet invents. He begins by deriving the word "poet" from the Greek *poiein,* "to make." He then shows that all human arts have nature as their principal object: "There is no art delivered unto mankind that hath not the works of nature for his principal object, without which they could not consist, and on which they so depend as they become actors and players, as it were, of what nature will have set forth." Among these arts Sidney includes astronomy, geometry, arithmetic, natural philosophy, grammar, rhetoric, logic, physics, and metaphysics. All of them

> build upon the depth of nature. Only the poet, disdaining to be tied to any such subjection, lifted up with the vigor of his own invention, doth grow in effect another nature, in making things either better than nature bringeth forth, or, quite anew, forms such as never were in nature, as the heroes, demigods, cyclops, chimeras, furies, and such like; so as he goeth hand in hand with nature, not enclosed within the narrow warrant of her gifts but freely ranging within the zodiac of his own wit. Nature never set forth the earth in so rich tapestry as divers poets have done, neither with so pleasant rivers, fruitful trees, sweet-smelling flowers, nor whatsoever else may make the too much loved earth more lovely. Her world is brazen, the poets only deliver a golden.

Sidney goes on to claim that the skill of the artist is seen in "that idea or fore-conceit of the work, and not in the work itself." This seems to throw the emphasis back upon the mental powers of the poet, upon what later writers will call the imagination, though oddly enough it may suggest only a new sort of imitation: the poem as an imitation of the imaginative products of the poet's mind. Nevertheless, it is a mistake to see Sidney as an anticipator of Romantic theories of the "creative imagination." His remark quoted above reflects a neo-Platonic attitude: The poet transcends lower nature.

Sidney's remarks and the problems of the Italians with imitation only presage a thoroughgoing revolution in critical thought that occurred concurrently with the development of scientific method and with the philosophical revolution separating nature into subjective and objective realms. This intellectual upheaval can be traced in the writings of such people as the astronomer Galileo Galilei (1564–1642) and the philosopher Francis Bacon (1561–1626). It is particularly codified in the "Discourse on Method" and the *Meditations* of René Descartes (1596–1650) and the "Essay Concerning Human Understanding" of John Locke (1632–1704). Starting from a complete skepticism and solipsism, Descartes asked what indeed it was possible to know and reasoned that he knew that he thought and that therefore he existed. Beyond that it became difficult to establish anything, but Descartes concluded that in mathematics there are grounds for a firm knowledge of things. The measurable became the objectively real.

Locke formalized the idea of the objective by distinguishing between the primary qualities of experience, those aspects of the object that demonstrably inhere in it by measurement, and the secondary qualities of experience that are impressed upon the object by the mind perceiving it. Included among the latter were the qualities of taste, touch, smell, color, sound, and so forth. To make this distinction was to call into question, as Descartes had recognized, the validity of direct human experience and to complicate immensely the relation of the mind to the so-called objects of its perception. Subsequent philosophers made various efforts to bring subject and object together again. George Berkeley (1685–1753), the Anglo-Irish philosopher, sought to reduce Locke's distinction to absurdity by arguing that since we perceive directly only by means of the secondary qualities, and if these are subjective, then we cannot ever prove that the object, composed of the real, primary qualities, exists at all. If one followed Locke's argument out to its end, one would have to conclude that the so-called material or objective world cannot be known, that there are no grounds for assuming its existence, and that it is an idea just as subjective as the secondary qualities were to Locke.

These ideas gave new meanings to the word "nature" and

new complexities.[10] As a result, also, the idea of art as imitation was greatly obfuscated and nearly eclipsed. The German philosopher Friedrich von Schelling (1775–1854) remarks of this turn of affairs:

> Has not indeed every theory of modern times taken its departure from this very position, that Art should be the imitator of Nature? Such has indeed been the case. But what should this broad general proposition profit the artist, when the notion of Nature is of such various interpretation, and when there are almost as many differing views of it as there are various modes of life? Thus, to one, Nature is nothing more than the lifeless aggregate of an indeterminable crowd of objects, or the space in which, as in a vessel, he imagines things placed; to another, only the soil from which he draws his nourishment and support; to the inspired seeker alone, the holy, ever-creative original energy of the world, which generates and busily evolves all things out of itself.[11]

Generally, literary theory under the influence of what the philosopher A. N. Whitehead called "the bifurcation of nature" split in two directions.[12] One of these, arising out of the emphasis upon empirical science, seems to find new meaning in Aristotle's observation that literature deals with universals rather than the particulars of history. Several eighteenth-century critics saw the artist copying not the minute particulars but arriving, through a process analogous to that of inductive generalization, at the true form of the object. Behind this also lay the Platonic idea of the forms as the true reality. The method now employed to achieve a true form was analogous to classification in the sciences.

This tendency is perhaps best illustrated by the artist Joshua Reynolds (1723–92) in his *Discourses*. He begins by insisting that the artist should not copy nature too closely: "There are excellencies in the art of painting beyond what is commonly called the imitation of nature." He complains about the artist who makes a fetish of the "minute neatness of his imitations." He goes on to argue, however, in the third *Discourse*:

[10] On the meanings of nature see A. O. Lovejoy, "Nature as an Aesthetic Norm" in *Essays in the History of Ideas* (New York: Putnam's 1960), pp. 69–77. Also A. N. Whitehead, *Science and the Modern World* (New York: New American Library, 1949) and Joseph Warren Beach, *The Concept of Nature in Nineteenth-Century English Poetry* (New York: Macmillan, 1936).

[11] From "On the Relations of the Plastic Arts to Nature," tr. by J. Elliott Cabot.

[12] See Whitehead, *op. cit., passim.*

> Thus it is from a reiterated experience, and a close comparison of the objects in nature, that an artist becomes possessed of that central form, if I may so express it, from which every deviation is deformity . . . . And as there is one general form, which, as I have said, belongs to the human kind at large, so in each of these classes there is one common idea and central form, which is the abstract of the various individual forms belonging to that class.

What Reynolds seems to be calling for is a sort of search for the Platonic idea of particular objects, but it also appears that he feels the idea is discoverable through a process of abstraction from experience, generalization from sense data, and isolation of the common elements of the species. Thus the portrait of a man must represent his humanity. One of the most interesting things about Neoclassical criticism is that it seems to mark a transition from the idea of the Platonic universal as the aim of art to the generalized abstraction.

This transition seems to be completed in the writings of the leading English critic of the age, Samuel Johnson (1709–84), particularly in *Rasselas,* where the language is clearly not Platonic:

> The business of the poet, said Imlac, is to examine, not the individual but the species; to remark general properties and large appearances: he does not number the streaks of the tulip, or describe the different shades in the verdure of the forest. He is to exhibit in his portraits of nature such prominent and striking features, as recall the original to every mind; and must neglect the minuter discriminations, which one may have remarked and another have neglected, for those characteristicks which are alike obvious to vigilance and carelessness.

The application of "method" gives a new meaning to imitation. Although the poet does not "number the streaks of the tulip" as might the scientist, he does, according to Johnson, proceed inductively to the "central form" by a process of generalization derived from scientific method. As a result, the nature he imitates is not so much what is apparent to his senses as what may be abstracted and generalized from them and found to inhere in all the objects of the class to which the particular belongs. This adoption of the language of inductive generalization enveloped literary criticism in a great fog, where it wandered for some time. Literary discussions occasionally lose themselves in the same fog even today. If there is a moral in this, perhaps it is that criticism should constantly examine its fundamental premises and its vocabulary and not allow itself to be bewitched by the language of the current science.

The new vocabulary was anathema to the poets and critics who, representing the second direction of theory, rejected the Lockean distinction between subject and object and the reality of generalizations. They felt generally that Locke's position tended to underestimate the meaningfulness of direct sensuous experience and to reduce the real to products of scientific investigation. Given the choice between Locke and Berkeley, they would at least find in Berkeley grounds for establishing the dignity of direct experience. William Blake's marginal notes to Reynolds' *Discourses* pointedly reject the reality of Reynolds' generalized abstractions and the so-called primary qualities of experience, which he classifies as simply abstractions from direct sensuous experience: "What is General Nature? is there Such a Thing? What is General Knowledge? is there such a Thing? Strictly Speaking All Knowledge is Particular."

Blake (1757–1827) goes so far as to reject the reality of nature if it is to be associated with the primary qualities of experience, that "sightless, soundless, scentless world" Whitehead describes as "merely the hurrying of matter, endlessly, meaninglessly." [13] Blake believes such a world to have been created by a satanic trinity, "Bacon, Newton, Locke"; in the marginalia to Reynolds he writes: "All Forms are Perfect in the Poet's Mind, but these are not Abstracted nor Compounded from Nature, but are from Imagination." By the time that Blake has come to Reynolds' *Eighth Discourse* he cannot resist a long note outlining his complaint and naming his villains, adding Edmund Burke to the list:

> Burke's Treatise on the Sublime & Beautiful is founded on the Opinions of Newton and Locke; on this Treatise Reynolds has grounded many of his assertions in all his Discourses. I read Burke's Treatise when very Young; at the same time I read Locke on Human Understanding & Bacon's Advancement of Learning; on Every one of these Books I wrote my Opinions, & on looking them over find that my Notes on Reynolds are exactly Similar. I felt the Same Contempt & Abhorrence then that I do now. They mock Imagination and Vision.

In his *Philosophical Inquiry into the Origin of Our Ideas of the Sublime and Beautiful* (1757), Burke (1729–97) had argued that the imagination is "incapable of producing anything ab-

---

[13] Whitehead, *op. cit.*, p. 80.

solutely new; it can only vary the disposition of those ideas which it has received from the senses." The major critics of the Romantic age, of whom Coleridge was probably the foremost theorist in England, would hold, first, that each new whole is more than the sum of its parts. Second, they would attribute to the imagination more radically creative powers than even the first principle implies. The Romantic movement is characterized by numerous assertions that the mind is at least partially consti- tutive of the reality it experiences. Behind many of these asser- tions lies the Kantian epistemology: Through the forms of space and time (the spectacles we can never remove) and the categories of understanding we build up the world, shape it according to our mental natures, bring intellectual order out of the manifold of sensation surrounding us.[14] This epistemological view forma- lizes a growing tendency to emphasize differences between art and nature, rather than their imitative relationship. Johnson remarked that when we go to a play we do not wish to be, indeed cannot be, fooled into thinking the action real (as a result he disagreed with Castelvetro about the unity of time). Immanuel Kant (1724–1804) would agree with Johnson on this point:

> In a product of beautiful art, we must become conscious that it is art and not nature; but yet the purposiveness of its form must seem to be as free from all constraint of arbitrary rules as if it were a product of mere nature . . . . Nature is beautiful because it looks like art, and art can only be beautiful if we are conscious of it as art while yet it looks like nature.[15]

The imitative relation between art and nature has not yet turned completely around, but it has begun to wheel. The re- lationship is now rather one of parallel inner forms than of outer appearances. The work of art has its own formal structure that is like that of nature. The parallel is not between the parts but between artistic objects and nature as a whole because they each are organic wholes. As Sidney observed, though with not quite the same meaning, the poet grows another nature.

The two directions already mentioned become more clearly delineated as the nineteenth century proceeds. On the one hand, the Romantic critics emphasized organic form and the creative powers of the mind. Their epistemology was essentially Kantian.

---

[14] Kant's position is laid out in the *Critique of Pure Reason* and in simplified form in the *Prolegomena to Any Future Metaphysics.*

[15] Immanuel Kant, *Critique of Judgment,* tr. by J. H. Bernard (New York: Hafner, 1951), p. 149.

On the other, the naturalists and realists emphasized a naive form of imitation. Their epistemology was essentially positivistic, traceable back to Locke and Descartes; knowledge was to come through scientific method. The French novelist Emile Zola (1840–1902) asserted in his famous essay "The Experimental Novel" (1893) that all the modes of human knowledge had little by little been driven into taking the path of science. Heavily influenced by Claude Bernard's *Introduction to the Study of Experimental Medicine,* he argued that the novelist was not merely an observer but an experimentalist. If experiment leads to a knowledge of the physical world, why, he contended, should it not reveal truths about the passions and the intellect? Experimental method "consists in finding the relations which unite a phenomenon of any kind to its nearest cause, or, in other words, in determining the conditions necessary for the manifestation of this phenomenon." [16] The observer takes in the phenomena as nature provides them; the experimentalist "employs the simple and complex process of investigation to vary or modify, for an end of some kind, the natural phenomena, and to make them appear under circumstances and conditions in which they are not presented in nature."

One wonders at first whether these ideas are so very different from Aristotle's, clothed as they may be in a scientific jargon: The artist takes forms from nature and presents them in a new matter. But this is quite far from what Zola means, for he is not concerned with the artistic matter, or medium, but only with situations:

> I will take as an example the character of the Baron Hulot, in *Cousine Bette,* by Balzac. The general fact observed by Balzac is the ravages that the amorous temperament of a man makes in his home, in his family, and in society. As soon as he has chosen his subject, he starts from known facts; then he makes his experiment, and exposes Hulot to a series of trials, placing him amid certain surroundings in order to exhibit how the complicated machinery of his passions works. It is then evident that there is not only observation there, but that there is also experiment; as Balzac does not remain satisfied with photographing the facts collected by him, but interferes in a direct way to place his character in certain conditions, and of these he remains the master.

Zola's vision of the novelist is, then, of one who takes a type of character from real life, observes it, places it in what might

[16] Quotations from Zola are from the translation by Belle Sherman.

be called a controlled atmosphere, then works out its inevitable actions. In controlling the atmosphere the novelist modifies nature, improves on it in a way, perhaps, but in a way quite different from what Sidney had in mind.

In Zola's description of Balzac's method we find an attitude similar to Reynolds'. Balzac reaches by observation an abstract idea of how human nature acts in a common situation. He then exploits this generalization by creating new situations. The addition Zola makes to Reynolds' idea lies in his sense of determinism, that the character will act in a certain way. The major weakness of the position is that the artist himself makes the new situations with a freedom the experimental scientist cannot attain. Further, it is *he* who commands the characters. Aristotle argued that in a play a person of a certain type should act as he probably would act; however, he allowed that a probable impossibility is not to be eschewed. It is superior to an improbable possibility. Playing with this paradox, we see that we might use it as a text in an argument against Zola's determinism. What makes something probable in art but impossible in life? How does a poet get away with such a thing? Perhaps he makes improbable and even impossible things probable or plausible by the artistic design he gives to them. The rules of plausibility in art and nature are perhaps different.

If this is so, then Zola has made too naive an equation between art and the observable world, or he has made too naive an equation between the way the artist abstracts the forms of his art from his experience and the way the scientist observes and experiments. If this is so, we see too why Aristotle was so careful to insist that it was more important to paint the hind artistically than to paint it without horns. Carried along on the crest of a theory that assumes the existence of a simple external reality and stresses adherence to it in art at the expense of everything else, the critic neglects the totality of art. He neglects particularly its medium.

One of the strongest polemicists for literary realism, the American novelist W. D. Howells (1837–1920) would argue, too, against the horned hind. Like that of any polemical critic, his impulse was to rebel against the literary values and excesses of a previous age. He attacked that separation from life brought about by the tendency of later Romantic writers to look not enough at nature and too much at the work of their predecessors. He insisted that the common, the average, man has the true standard of arts in his power, though he avoided the problem of finding an average man who could deliver the canons of taste to him. This idea of typicality tends to undermine many of the sensible things Howells had to say. Not only did he hypothesize a typical reader, but he also espoused typicality of subject matter, which tended to reduce nature to generalized abstractions. Oddly enough, in Howells the realist, nature becomes a sort of fiction. Scientific method again invades art.

At the same time that the cry to return to nature and, by implication, to copy it faithfully (and perhaps scientifically) was heard, so was the opposite, the insistence that nature is dull:

> In recent years we have heard it said in a thousand different ways, "Copy nature; only copy nature. There is no greater delight, no finer triumph than an excellent copy of nature." And this doctrine (the enemy of art) was alleged to apply not only to painting but to all the arts, even to the novel and to poetry.

Charles Baudelaire (1821–67), who offered these remarks in a piece of art criticism in 1859, goes on to insist: "It is useless and tedious to represent what *exists*, because nothing that *exists* satisfies me." Baudelaire announces that he prefers "the monsters of my fancy to what is positively trivial." But even more fundamental is the following consideration:

> it would have been more philosophical to ask the doctrinaires in question first of all whether they were quite certain of the existence of external nature, or (if this question might seem too well calculated to pander to their sarcasm) whether they were quite certain of knowing *all nature*.[17]

The question is not a foolish one. Indeed it is the question that has grown steadily in its implications through this brief history. When Aristotle proposed imitation he did not ask Baudelaire's embarrassing question, for it was not conceivable as a question. If we look at the Sophoclean trilogy, which became the model for his dramatic theory, we discover certain assumptions about the structure of life or nature that Aristotle apparently accepted without critical reflection. Recent research that reveals possible ritual origins for Greek tragedy suggests that the Greeks must have accepted or thought in the forms of the rhythm of life that these rituals and myths implied.[18] Broad

---

[17] Charles Baudelaire, *The Mirror of Art*, tr. and ed. by Jonathan Mayne (New York: Doubleday, 1956), pp. 233–34.
[18] See Francis Fergusson, *Idea of a Theater: A Study of Ten Plays* (New York: Doubleday, 1953), for critical applications of a principle implicit in anthro-

patterns of action in Greek drama are then not merely artificial constructions but were regarded as the very structure of life and human action itself—nature.

This sense of what was being imitated is certainly less clear among Renaissance critics, and the whole problem of imitation reached a new crisis with the further development of empiricism and the split of nature into subject and object. When science labels only the objective world as nature, writers like Blake and Baudelaire reject nature. For them it is a fiction; such things as typicality and the average mean nothing to them. It is not, of course, that nature does not exist for them in any sense; they only reject nature defined as Locke's primary qualities of experience.

The two directions taken by criticism in the nineteenth century are clearly opposed. Tacitly accepting science's capture of objectivity, many critics and writers retreated into the subjective. It was an uneasy retreat, and they left themselves unprotected from the realists, who accused them of isolation from life. On the other hand, as I have already observed, when the realists justified their art on some analogy with scientific method, it came to be seen that the primary, or objective, world was as abstract and as difficult to locate as the Romantic unrealities they despised. Apparently art had to be examined without any assumption that either the objective or the subjective was the ultimate ground of knowledge. The language of Locke was inadequate.

Curiously this effort seems to have arisen from the subjectivist direction rather than the objectivist. Or perhaps this is not so curious considering that for centuries critics had struggled with the idea that art copies a given reality. It is, therefore, back to the first subjectivists, the Romantics, and then to the Symbolists, and to the exponents of *Art pour l'art* that we must go to trace the development of that modern criticism that seeks to dispense with the terms "objective" and "subjective."

The so-called objectivist operates upon nature or whatever by a process of abstraction toward generalization. On the other

---

pological studies by the Cambridge school of anthropologists. For earlier studies see Gilbert Murray, *The Rise of the Greek Epic,* 4th ed. (New York: Oxford Univ. Press, 1960), and "Hamlet and Orestes" in his *The Classical Tradition in Poetry* (New York: Random House, 1957), and Jessie Weston, *From Ritual to Romance* (New York: Doubleday, 1957). A fundamental anthropological study is Jane Ellen Harrison's *Epilegomena to the Study of Greek Religion* (New Hyde Park, N.Y.: University Books, 1962).

hand, the subjectivist is concerned with the concrete experience in its immediacy. Let us begin study of the gradual effort to escape this dichotomy with Johann Wolfgang von Goethe's conversations. "Do not imagine all is vanity, if it is not abstract thought and idea," Goethe observes in the *Conversations with Eckerman*. He then adds: "It was, on the whole, not in my line, as a poet, to strive to embody anything *abstract*. I received in my mind impressions, and those of a sensual, animated, charming, varied, hundredfold kind, just as a lively imagination presented them."

Goethe (1749–1832) developed a distinction between allegory and symbolism that cropped up over and over in the Romantic age: The allegorist begins with an abstract idea like love, beauty, or courage and translates it into a concrete image—Venus, a rose, a lion. Its implicit meaning is still love, beauty, courage, or whatever. Goethe rejects allegory and praises the symbolic. A symbol does not have an abstract idea implicit in it, and it is not translatable. Now since abstract ideas are the food of the understanding, which is an analytic power, and all interpretation naturally moves toward the abstract, Goethe can assert: "I am rather of the opinion that the more incommensurable, and the more incomprehensible to the intellect, a poetic production is, so much the better it is."

These remarks form part of the struggle to draw a distinction between art and scientific or logical modes of discourse that continues into the New Criticism of the twentieth century. An example along the way is Paul Valéry's essay "Poetry and Abstract Thought." Valéry (1871–1945) begins his essay somewhat skeptical of the distinction implied in his title, thinking it not so hard and fast as Goethe made it. But he goes on to espouse it himself. He says that some utterances are like walking to a destination; the achievement of the destination is what counts. The language used to achieve the destination is rendered unimportant or even meaningless (it is destroyed, so to speak) by the achievement. Thus if I ask you for a light and you give me a light, the destination is reached and the language has performed its function. The words are destroyed or transformed into nonlanguage, which in this case is the reception of the light:

> in practical or abstract uses of language, the form—that is the physical, the concrete part, the very act of speech—does not last; it does not outlive understanding; it dissolves in the light; it has acted; it has done its work; it has brought about understanding; it has lived.

What, however, if some statements are not exhausted? "On the other hand, the moment this concrete form takes on, by an effect of its own, such importance that it asserts itself and makes itself, as it were, respected; and not only remarked and respected, but desired and therefore repeated—then something new happens." Here rather than walking toward a destination there is something going on more like a dance, which circles back upon itself. It is going nowhere: "The poem . . . does not die for having lived: it is expressly designed to be born again from its ashes and to become endlessly what it has been." [19]

Many writers have also argued that art does not, like science, improve. Einsteinian physics was an improvement over Newtonian. Newton greatly improved on Thales. But to say that the art of the ancient Greeks is better or worse than our own seems pointless. In talking of earlier physics, incidentally, it is much easier to use the past tense than in talking about ancient Greek drama, which is still present to us. The reason for our refusal to say that art improves is related to Goethe's and Valéry's arguments. Physics posits a destination in Valéry's terms, and it is abstract and ideational in Goethe's. Having no destination, art cannot be termed obsolete for falling short. The sort of improvement noticeable in physics cannot possibly be discovered in art and is irrelevant to its value.

We notice that Goethe's remarks reflect the point of view of the artist and his aims, while Valéry seems more concerned with the art object itself as we contemplate it. In fact, his whole point is that rather than receiving a communication from the artist through it (with the result that we can burn the letter, so to speak), we contemplate and recontemplate the object. The shift of vantage from that of Goethe to that of Valéry is part of the history of nineteenth-century criticism. Observing the matter from Goethe's point of view, John Keats proposed in a famous letter his definition of "negative capability": "at once it struck me what quality went to form a Man of Achievement, especially in Literature & which Shakespeare possessed so enormously—I mean *Negative Capability,* that is when a man is capable of being in uncertainties, Mysteries, doubts, without any irritable reaching after fact & reason." [20] Keats, of course, did not know Shakespeare personally. He was talking about a quality that he thought Shakespeare must have had as a person, given the nature of his plays.

[19] From *The Art of Poetry,* tr. by Denise Folliot, Vol. VII of Paul Valéry, *Collected Works,* ed. by Jackson Matthews (New York: Bollingen Series, 1958).
[20] Letter to George and Thomas Keats, December 22, 1818.

Practically speaking, however, he was saying something about the plays themselves, namely that they are successful *because* they do not seem to be insisting on the communication of some abstract doctrine. They are not vehicles for ideas that can be abstracted from them. They are, in Valéry's terms, a dance. Therefore, if art copies nature, following Keats's point of view it must not copy by generalizing but by presenting experience directly and concretely. He complained about Coleridge in this matter: "Coleridge, for instance, would let go by a fine isolated verisimilitude caught from the Penetralium of mystery, from being incapable of remaining content with half knowledge." But Coleridge, too, was wary of the tendency Keats observes in him. One might recall here Coleridge's own reply to Mrs. Barbauld, who could find no moral in "The Rime of the Ancient Mariner." Coleridge answered that the opposite was the case; the moral sentiment was obtruded too openly upon the reader. The poem was in danger of being read as a tract, of being viewed as a walk toward a destination.

This view leads writers of many sorts to play down what might be called the subject matter of a literary work. The artist begins to associate subject matter with, first, that which can be generalized up and out of primary nature and, second, with an abstractable idea or message. Since he believes that a literary work should not be a conveyor of an abstraction, he asserts that it has no subject matter. Gustave Flaubert (1821–80) is well known for remarks of this sort. He wished to write "a book about nothing." [21] The plot, he insisted, was of no interest to him. He hated the idea of the presence of the author in his work. The author should be felt everywhere but seen nowhere. In Flaubert's terms, to be seen is to be "communicating with the reader. Yet, to be felt is to be present in all parts of the work, like the dancer of William Butler Yeats's famous poem "Among School Children":

> O body swayed to music, O brightening glance,
> How can we know the dancer from the dance?

Perhaps now we can easily separate some key words into two columns.

| | |
|---|---|
| abstraction (generalization) | concretion |
| scientific method | art |
| logic | intuition, imagination |
| discourse (communication) | presentation |
| thought | negative capability |

[21] See Flaubert's letter to Louise Colet, 1852.

| | |
|---|---|
| walking | dancing |
| ideas | style |
| allegory | symbolism |

Toward the end of the nineteenth century, the essay "The Decay of Lying" by Oscar Wilde (1854–1900) relates these ideas to the idea of imitation, inverting the statement that art imitates and insisting that nature imitates art. At the same time, however, Wilde turns to Aristotle. The essay is a dialogue between two gentlemen, Cyril and Vivian, in the library of a Nottinghamshire country house. Cyril suggests that they remove themselves to the terrace to smoke cigarettes and enjoy nature. Vivian declines, arguing that he does not enjoy nature:

> My own experience is that the more we study Art, the less we care for Nature. What Art really reveals to us is Nature's lack of design, her curious crudities, her extraordinary monotony, her absolutely unfinished condition. Nature has good intentions, of course, but, as Aristotle once said, she cannot carry them out.

It is clear that Wilde and Aristotle agree on some points, even though Wilde rejects imitation. The imitation Wilde rejects is, of course, not Aristotle's but the kind implied by a modern naive realism. Wilde goes boldly beyond Aristotle to formulate these doctrines:

1. Art never expresses anything but itself.
2. All bad Art comes from returning to Life and Nature and elevating them into ideals.
3. Life imitates Art far more than Art imitates Life. A corollary to this is that external Nature also imitates Art.
4. Lying, the telling of beautiful untrue things, is the proper aim of Art.

The first doctrine arises from the same attitude that turned Goethe against abstraction, that is, it assumes that discursive generalization is the mode of *saying* something to someone and that art does not use language in this way. Doctrine 2 is a direct attack upon the theoretical position of naturalists and realists, who adopt modes of generalization, confusing artistic method with scientific method. Doctrine 4 ironically uses the word "lying" in a sense acceptable to the realist. The third doctrine properly stands near the conclusion of our brief history of imitation, as Wilde gleefully knew it must; here the epistemology that begins with Kant is worked to the limit. Art tends to create nature:

Where, if not from the Impressionists, do we get those wonderful brown fogs that come creeping down our streets, blurring the gas-lamps and changing the houses into monstrous shadows? To whom, if not to them and their master, do we owe the lovely silver mists that brood over our river, and turn to faint forms of fading grace the curved bridge and the swaying barge? The extraordinary change that has taken place in the climate of London during the last ten years is entirely due to a particular school of Art. You smile. Consider the matter from a scientific or a metaphysical point of view, and you will find that I am right.

Wilde never insists that nothing is out there, but he does insist that we give shape to meaningless, inchoate nature, the manifold of sensation, by our art. In Wilde, the Aristotelian idea of art surpassing nature is reasserted. He is not combating Aristotle; it is the naturalists and realists who are his enemy. He allies himself with the Aristotelian emphasis upon form and structure.

Literature is composed of words; Wilde's position implies that nature imitates words or systems of words. If we look around us, we recognize that all systems of symbols are not composed of words. Music is a system of symbols; so is mathematics. In a quite different way Plato came close to the idea that nature copies mathematics. Twentieth-century critical theory is often charac-terized by discussions of systems or families of symbols, each based on different interior principles of order, each organizing or schematizing nature in its own way. The epistemological shift set in motion by Kant reaches completion in this century in the sort of observation made by Ernst Cassirer:

> Like all other symbolic forms art is not the mere reproduction of a ready-made, given reality. It is one of the ways leading to an objective view of things and of human life. It is not an imitation but a discovery of reality. We do not, however, discover nature through art in the same sense in which the scientist uses the term "nature" . . . . Language[22] and science are abbreviations of reality. Language and science depend upon one and the same process of abstraction; art may be described as a continuous process of concretion.[23]

[22] Cassirer uses the term here to mean language in its discursive, logical func-tion.

[23] Ernst Cassirer, *An Essay on Man* (New Haven, Conn.: Yale Univ. Press, 1944), pp. 143–44. See also *Language and Myth* (New York: Dover, 1946), and *The Philosophy of Symbolic Forms,* 3 vols. (New Haven, Conn.: Yale Univ. Press, 1953–57) by the same author.

Cassirer is insisting not on the subjectivity of the artist but on the objectivity. Actually he is denying the former meanings of these words and the way experience was divided by the tradition in which Locke wrote. Cassirer sharpens his distinction:

> In our scientific description of a given object we begin with a great number of observations which at first sight are only a loose conglomerate of detached facts. But the farther we proceed the more these individual phenomena tend to assume a definite shape and become a systematic whole. What science is searching for is some central feature of a given object from which all its particular qualities may be derived. If a chemist knows the atomic number of a certain element he possesses a clue to a full insight into its structure and constitution. From this number he may deduce all the characteristic properties of the element. But art does not admit of this sort of conceptual simplification and deductive generalization. It does not inquire into the qualities or causes of things; it gives us the intuition of the form of things. But this too is by no means a mere repetition of something we had before. It is a true and genuine discovery. The artist is just as much a discoverer of the forms of nature as the scientist is a discoverer of facts or natural laws.[24]

Thus art is made a symbolic form with its own principles, a discoverer of reality as it is shaped and in a sense created by the principles.

Another aspect of imitation remains to be mentioned. It is the dictum of Horace (65–8 B.C.) that the artist is wise to imitate his great predecessors. This idea, which appears in the *Ars Poetica,* has been widely applied and interpreted. Perhaps two applications of it by famous poets will illustrate its most interesting aspect. The first is from Alexander Pope's "Essay on Criticism" (1711), the second from T. S. Eliot's essay "Tradition and the Individual Talent" (1917):

> When first young Maro in his boundless mind
> A work to outlast immortal Rome design'd,
> Perhaps he seem'd above the critic's law,
> And but from Nature's fountains scorn'd to draw:
> But when to examine every part he came,
> Nature and Homer were, he found, the same.

If we approach a poet without this prejudice we shall often find that not only the best, but the most individual parts of his work

[24] *Ibid.,* p. 143.

may be those in which the dead poets, his ancestors, assert their immortality most vigorously.[25]

Pope (1688–1744) was, we suppose, insisting on the power of Homer to imitate nature in the Aristotelian sense, even to improve upon it perhaps, and not simply to imitate its content but its form. Pope implies that Homer's success was so remarkable that to copy Homer ever since has inevitably been to appear to copy nature. In the light of our discussion a rationale for Pope's argument has emerged that may be stronger than any Pope may have imagined.

If, as Cassirer suggests, art discovers or makes nature, or a symbolic form for it, then nature is in some sense contained in art. The new artist will, in shaping nature, shape it inevitably according to the conventions implicit in his art. This is to say that a work of art is recognizable as such, just as a mathematical formula is recognizable from the conventions it uses. For this reason it is difficult and perhaps quite undesirable to escape imitating Homer.

Eliot (1888–1965) carries the same idea further, insisting that real individuality occurs in poetry when the poet most intensively cements his relationship to poets of the past. Eliot is attacking the cliché of originality that arose with romantic subjectivism. At that time poets sought an excuse for their existence in the face of scientific modes of knowledge. With the establishment of art as an independent symbolic mode, originality ceases to be demanded—at least in quite the same sense.

Our history of imitation and creation does not really end here. These two words and the ideas surrounding them thread themselves through all the subsequent chapters. Furthermore, we cannot discuss the present situation of criticism without returning to them. This we shall do in Chapter 6.

[25] T. S. Eliot, *Selected Essays 1917–1932* (New York: Harcourt, Brace & World, 1932), p. 4.

# 3 DELIGHT, DIDACTICISM, AND THERAPY

Criticism has always had to deal with the relation between the literary work and its audience. It was an issue with Plato, and many interpreters think it enters into Aristotle's remark about catharsis. After Plato and Aristotle perhaps the most famous early comments upon the aims of poetry with respect to its audience occur in the *Ars Poetica,* or *Epistle to the Pisos,* of Horace (65–8 B.C.). He writes, "The aim of the poet is to inform or delight, or to combine together, in what he says, both pleasure and applicability to life. He who combines the useful and the pleasing wins out by both instructing and delighting the reader." Subsequent critics have taken Horace's cue and attributed to literature the power to teach the reader, delight him, move him, or act therapeutically upon him. The other side of the coin is that ever since Plato there have been continued attacks upon literature voicing the fear that it teaches things unsuitable to the young or even to the middle-aged.

No one except a professor disillusioned by a bad hour in the classroom has ever seriously asserted that literature does not affect the reader in some way or another. However, many critics, particularly those of the twentieth century, have indicated that (1) the problem of the relation of literature to the audience is secondary to more fundamental problems and (2) the relation between work and reader is so full of variables that it is impossible to make any meaningful generalization about what literature does. The problem of variables goes back at least to Aristotle. Although he has often been interpreted as mentioning the cathartic effect of tragedy and pleasure as an end of art, he clearly does not believe that pleasure or any other reaction in the audience can adequately define the work itself. It is apparently something that does arise when the work is successful, but that is only a "sign of success in the participant or beholder." [1] As a result, it appears impossible to arrive at a judgment of value by examining the relationship empirically. Both of these complaints are strong ones; yet speculation about the effect of literature and attempts to develop theories of value on the basis of its effect continue. Sometimes a critic concerned with literature's imitative function will berate a critic interested in its didactic or therapeutic function when the fact is that these critics are not disagreeing so much as observing the object from totally different vantages. On the other hand, such critics are usually in serious disagreement as to what is most important about a literary work and about literary values generally. Furthermore, critics fairly conscientious about keeping to a single point of view sometimes shift vantages without being aware that they do.[2]

One of the earliest assertions about literature is that it teaches the reader or that it sets some sort of example to be followed. For Plato, literature set a bad example because of its irrationality and therefore subversive nature. At the other pole, literature has been praised because it teaches moral truths that are arrived at by rational means. Critics have also inverted these assumptions. They have praised literature *because* it is irrational or because it is subversive of the opinions of the establishment, and they have attacked some kinds of literature because they have too openly taught.[3]

Beyond the moral realm, literature has been considered a conveyor of information—social, psychological, historical, scientific—while some critics have insisted on the aesthetic irrelevance of its informational function. This debate is an old one going back to the early discussion in Aristotle of whether Empedocles was or was not a poet. Aristotle conceded that Empedocles wrote in verse but noted that he did not make plots. In fact, Empedocles was concerned only with the conveyance of scientific information. In recent times the question has been

---

[1] See R. S. Crane, *The Languages of Criticism and the Structure of Poetry* (Toronto: Univ. of Toronto Press, 1953), p. 59.
[2] For a discussion of this from a neo-Aristotelian point of view see Elder Olson, "An Outline of Poetic Theory" in R. S. Crane, ed., *Critics and Criticism* (Chicago: Univ. of Chicago Press, 1952), pp. 546–66.
[3] I think here of the sort of everyday criticism that implies a complete divorce between the didactic and the pleasurable in art, arguing that somehow the didactic must take away from the pleasure.

put as follows, Is a poem a conveyor of information, or is it an object about which we gather knowledge?

The first extant proposal that literature (specifically drama) performs a therapeutic function has been thought to be Aristotle's remark about tragic catharsis, or purgation. Most interpreters have argued that for Aristotle the audience benefits "through pity and fear effecting the proper purgation of these emotions." Whether this is what Aristotle meant or not, this interpretation has had an enormous influence into quite recent times. Even should we assume it to be correct, it appears to be the least fundamental part of his definition of tragedy. With the development of modern psychology a variety of therapeutic effects has been attributed to literature. Lionel Trilling has inferred from Freud's essay "Beyond the Pleasure Principle" a mithridatic or homeopathic function in tragedy.[4] I. A. Richards has proposed that poetry effects a balancing of emotions.[5] Several critics interested in anthropology and the relation of literature to myth have found social values in this relationship. Several problems face these critics, however. At what level of reading does therapy occur? In fact, what evidence can be produced that therapy occurs at all? What role does artistic technique play? Is *Little Orphan Annie* possibly more therapeutic than *Ulysses*?

Finally, of course, it has been a commonplace that literature delights or pleases or that it should delight or please. It is unfortunately true, however, that poems judged excellent by some for this reason have bored or even offended others and perhaps mystified even more. It is possible that literary delight comes from moral agreement or having been morally persuaded. Perhaps delight comes with therapy or even upon the satisfactory solution of a puzzle. The problem here, however, is more complicated than simply recognizing the attachment of delight either to learning or to therapy. People are delighted by many things. Who is the universal reader? Or is the critic saying only that the reader ought to be delighted?

The traditional complaint against poets is made on moral grounds: The poet discusses or presents matters that are better left unmentioned; the poet tells lies; the poet is an irrationalist and misleads his readers. Plato's is the classic complaint. He carried his argument into the realm of practicality:

[4] Lionel Trilling, "Freud and Literature" in *The Liberal Imagination* (Garden City, N.Y.: Doubleday, 1953), pp. 44–64.
[5] See *Principles of Literary Criticism* (New York: Harcourt, Brace & World, 1925).

As in a city when the evil are permitted to wield power and the finer men are put out of the way, so in the soul of each man, as we shall maintain, the imitative poet implants an evil constitution, for he indulges the irrational nature which has no discernment of greater and less, but thinks the same thing at one time great and at another small—he is an imitator of images and is very far removed from the truth.[6]

Furthermore, the poet "feeds and waters the passions instead of drying them up." Plato objects strenuously to this because in his opinion the passions ought to be controlled or else man will never increase his happiness or his virtue. (Aristotle's idea of purgation is perhaps an answer to Plato here.)

In these remarks Plato seems to allow no middle ground between strict rationality and pure animal feeling. He is concerned lest the poet reduce everything to the test of hedonic pleasure and pain. He insists that only poems that are hymns to the gods or praise of great men may be admitted to the state: "If you go beyond this and allow the honeyed Muse to enter, either in epic or lyric verse, not law and the reason of mankind, which by common consent have ever been deemed best, but pleasure and pain will be the rulers in our State." Apologists for poetry have always had to take account of this sort of objection. Some have even used other remarks by Plato to defend themselves against his attacks. Renaissance Italian critics often made Platonic defenses of poetry. In England, Philip Sidney enumerated in the "Defence of Poesie" the traditional complaints against the poets before trying to refute them:

First, that there being many other more fruitful knowledges, a man might better spend his time in them than in this. Secondly, that it is the mother of lies. Thirdly, that it is the nurse of abuse, infecting us with many pestilent desires, with a siren's sweetness, drawing the mind to the serpent's tale of sinful fancies . . . . And lastly and chiefly, they cry out with open mouth, as if they had outshot Robin Hood, that Plato banished them out of his commonwealth.

Many writers took Plato's complaint that poetry aims at pleasure and turned it into praise. From Horace through Longinus to Sidney, critics generally averred that poetry aims to delight. They usually combined this assertion with arguments for a didactic function or some other usefulness. Occasionally a critic

---

[6] Quotations from Plato are from the translation by Benjamin Jowett in his *The Dialogues of Plato*, 4th ed. (Oxford, Eng.: Clarendon Press, 1953).

would extend the idea of delight to transport, as in the treatise *On The Sublime* (*c.* A.D. 80) attributed to Longinus: "it is not to persuasion but to ecstasy that passages of extraordinary genius carry the hearer: now the marvellous, with its power to amaze, is always and necessarily stronger than that which seeks to persuade and to please." [7] Generally, though, it was not until the eighteenth century, when Longinus became particularly fashionable, that ecstasy transcending both delight and teaching was considered a purpose of art.

Sidney's famous essay is a sort of compendium of the delight-and-teach principle. Poetry teaches by imitating the "inconceivable excellence of God," by dealing with philosophical matters, and by presenting histories. Sidney argues that because the poet does delight, he is a more effective teacher than the historian or the philosopher. Often, because goodness does not seem particularly attractive, the poet can "move men to take that goodness in hand, which without delight they would fly as from a stranger." The poet, then, offers "a sweet prospect into the way."

Italian predecessors of Sidney found various merits in the combination of delight and didacticism. Giovanni Boccaccio (1313–75), holding that poetry and theology were essentially the same, believed that the allegorical element in poetry made the theological lesson more pleasing because the meaning is "acquired with labor and therefore better retained." [8] On the other hand, Lodovico Castelvetro argued that not difficulty but ease of understanding is the effect of poetry, which is able "to delight and recreate the minds of the crude multitude and of the common people, who do not understand the reasons and the divisions and the arguments, subtle and far from the practice of ordinary men, which the philosophers use in investigating the truth of things." [9]

Castelvetro's argument is not really that people are taught by literature but that they are entertained and kept in line. Boccaccio's less cynical, Spartan view is the one more commonly voiced. Poetry is useful and the delight that comes from it serves as a means to ethical knowledge and moral betterment. Both arguments, however, answer or seem to answer Plato's challenge in their assertion that poetry "is pleasant but also useful to States and to human life."

[7] The quotation from Longinus's *On The Sublime* is from the translation by A. O. Prickard (1906).

[8] From *Vita de Dante* (1363–64).

[9] Quotations from Castelvetro's *Poetica d'Aristotele, vulgarizzita et sposta* (1576) are from the translation by Allan Gilbert in his *Literary Criticism: Plato to Dryden* (Detroit: Wayne State Univ. Press, 1962), pp. 305–57.

But with all this said, we notice among these same critics who answer Plato an idea that would have disturbed Plato immensely and probably given him grounds to send the poet on his way after all. Sidney claims that even though poetry teaches, it is primarily concerned with moving the passions. The philosopher, he says, cannot move the reader nearly as deeply: "And that moving is of a higher degree than teaching, it may by this appear, that it is wellnigh the cause and the effect of teaching."

Now according to Aristotle's definition, one of the elements of tragedy, though admittedly a lesser one, is catharsis. Aristotle was traditionally interpreted to have held that a perfect tragedy should "imitate" actions that excite pity and fear. His is usually taken to be the first literary theory to attribute therapeutic effect to art. The pleasure he is thought to have attributed to tragedy comes about by more complex means than the delight spoken of by Renaissance critics. Purgation is not the only pleasure. The imitation itself is pleasurable, and it is connected to learning: "the reason why men enjoy seeing a likeness is that in contemplating it they find themselves learning or inferring, and saying perhaps, 'Ah, that is he.' " [10] Aristotle goes on to remark that if one happens not to have seen the original, the pleasure comes from the way the artist has done things.

Renaissance critics like Antonio Minturno (1500–74) take the idea of the audience's purgation and encompass it by the didactic, moralistic function. Minturno says the poet teaches, delights, and moves. Tragedy shows us through the fall of great men that we must guard against evil, face adversity with patience, and not put our trust in worldly things. As tragedy does this, besides pleasing us with verse, ornament, spectacle, and so forth, it "arouses passion in the mind and induces astonishment in it, both filling it with horror and moving it to pity." [11] Curiously, because this horror and pity delight us, they purge us of these passions: "A physician will not have greater capacity to expel with poisonous medicine the fiery poison of an illness which afflicts the body, than the tragic poet will to purge the mind of mighty perturbations with the force of the passions charmingly expressed in verse." Minturno's view of tragedy is really a mithridatic one. The cure is effected in a Spartan manner, the audience becoming inured to suffering. There is a moral twist to all of this:

[10] Quotations from Aristotle are from the translation by S. H. Butcher in his *Aristotle's Theory of Poetry and Fine Art*, 4th ed. (New York: Dover, 1951).
[11] Quotations from Minturno's *L'arte poetica* (1564) are from the translation by Gilbert, *op. cit.*, pp. 275–303.

Yet this horror and this pity by delighting us purge us from like passions, because more than anything else they restrain the untamed fury of the human soul, for no one is so overcome by unrestrained appetites that if he is moved by fear and pity for the unhappiness of another his soul is not purged of the passions which have been the cause of that unhappy state.

Minturno also claims that tragedy has this moral use because it never presents anything that cannot actually come to pass. The view of Aristotle is converted to a moralistic and didactic one. Perhaps Giraldi Cinthio (1504–73) reduces it to its most succinct expression: "The function then of our poet, with respect to affecting morals, is to praise virtuous actions and to blame vices and by means of the terrible and the piteous to make them odious to the reader." [12]

The problem raised somewhat innocently and certainly obliquely by Minturno comes back to haunt criticism in the eighteenth century. It is the problem of making tragedies that are probable or lifelike and that inevitably bring about the downfall of the wicked. It arises from the possible conflict between two kinds of didacticism: teaching what *is* and teaching what *ought to be*.

Sensing this problem, perhaps, and sensing that a definition of poetry in terms of its didactic function does not sufficiently distinguish it from philosophy or history, Castelvetro returned to Aristotle's insistence upon the primacy of plot:

Plot is final and not a thing accessory to the morals of the agents, but on the contrary the morals do not hold the final place and are accessory to the plot . . . . In addition, it would happen that if such material were principal and not accessory, it could not be poetic material, since it is naturally philosophical.

This is why Aristotle did not treat literature as didactic, having separated it from history and philosophy. It is as if one is driven back into the structure of the work in order to find its unique literary nature. This is also, perhaps, why after much struggle with its didactic function, Jacopo Mazzoni insists that poetry puts delight first. Then he concludes that moral and educational benefits are finally only fortunate by-products of the author's having made exactness of the image his sole aim.

The development of philosophical empiricism and its attention to problems of perception often turned Neoclassical critical interests to the problem of taste. "Taste," defined by Joseph Addison (1672–1719) as "that Faculty of the Soul, which discerns the Beauties of an Author with Pleasure and the Imperfections with Dislike," [13] is related to the term "aesthetics." Since Alexander Gottlieb Baumgarten in his *Aesthetica* used it in the eighteenth century to mean the science of perception or sensuous knowledge, it has come to be associated nearly exclusively with art. The problem of an empirical approach to value in art—to discover some solid, unchanging principle of judgment in the viewer—has already been touched upon. In the eighteenth century, the word "taste" became the convenient repository of this mystery.

In his essay "Of the Standard of Taste" (1757) the empirical philosopher David Hume (1711–76) puts the issue squarely before us by insisting that beauty is in the beholder, not in the object; but he tries to save mankind from complete anarchic impressionism by asserting that there is a uniformity in human nature that leads us to standards of taste:

> amidst all the variety and caprice of taste, there are certain general principles of approbation or blame, whose influence a careful eye may trace in all operations of the mind. Some particular forms or qualities, from the original structure of the internal fabric, are calculated to please, and others to displease; and if they fail of their effect in any particular instance, it is from some apparent defect or imperfection in the organ.

Hume implies that often our rules of art do not conform to our experience of pleasure and that when this is true the rules are proved false. Rules must be founded upon "experience and on the observation of the common sentiments of human nature." On the other hand, the mind is a delicate instrument and under many conditions cannot be expected to react to art according to its own laws of activity. The test of art can occur only under certain conditions, when the mind is properly receptive. It is clear also, Hume remarks, that delicacy of taste is improved by experience and practice. Someone with no experience in artistic matters, even though he suffers from no "apparent defect or imperfection in the organ," is not qualified to pronounce upon art. Further, there is the problem of the various prejudices that may invade a critical judgment. These must be avoided, of course. When all is said, it is difficult to find the proper judge:

[13] Joseph Addison, "Concerning the Development of Fine Taste," *Spectator*, No. 409, June 19, 1712.

The organs of internal sensation are seldom so perfect as to allow the general principles their full play, and produce a feeling correspondent to those principles. They either labour under some defect, or are vitiated by some disorder; and by that means excite a sentiment, which may be pronounced erroneous. When the critic has no delicacy, he judges without any distinction, and is only affected by the grosser and more palpable qualities of the object: The finer touches pass unnoticed and disregarded. Where he is not aided by practice, his verdict is attended with confusion and hesitation. Where no comparison has been employed, the most frivolous beauties, such as rather merit the name of defects, are the object of his admiration. Where he lies under the influence of prejudice, all his natural sentiments are perverted. Where good sense is wanting, he is not qualified to discern the beauties of design and reasoning, which are the highest and most excellent. Under some or other of these imperfections, the generality of men labour; and hence a true judge in the finer arts is observed, even during the most polished ages, to be so rare a character: Strong sense, united to delicate sentiment, improved by practice, perfected by comparison and cleared of all prejudice, can alone entitle critics to this valuable character; and the joint verdict of such, wherever they are to be found, is the true standard of taste and beauty.

As if enough problems have not already been enumerated, Hume reminds us that there are differences of judgment among men of different years of age, different eras, and different countries. It is as if Hume has destroyed the possibility of criticism just as he systematically destroyed causation in his philosophy.

Hume acknowledges that if a true critic could be found no one would deny his value. Wanting perfection in this matter, men must do the best they can. They should acknowledge that a "true standard of taste and beauty" does exist somewhere, and they should seek to approach it by formulating the truest principles of which they are capable. Hume, then, by no means despairs in this matter but points out that although theoretically standards are difficult to establish, men have consistently agreed in their judgments on artistic greatness, more so in fact than on other matters. The Latin poets Terence and Virgil remain in high esteem, while the value of philosophers fluctuates with the times and science constantly changes.

Hume's position arises as a result of the separation of experience into the subjective and objective. He insists that in matters of taste everything must be referred back to how we know. To build up standards of value one must examine the reader, since standards are referable to people, not to the works themselves. This is not to say that literary objects exist only in our minds. There may be no color, taste, or sound in objects, as Locke's distinction implies, but there is something in the nature of the object that causes us to ascribe particular secondary qualities to it. The same holds true, one supposes, of literary objects. Hume's insistence is that a rational discussion of art must begin as a discussion of human response, but his essay is finally most valuable as an introduction to the serious difficulties of examining literature from the point of view of the reader's response.

No eighteenth-century critic wholly escaped the empirical predicament. The third Earl of Shaftesbury (1671–1713), who was influenced by a variety of philosophers and cannot be called rigidly empirical in the manner of Locke and Hume, was deeply concerned with the variations of human response.[14] Shaftesbury discusses idiosyncratic personal reactions even as he builds up the idea of objective judgment. Another theorist, Edmund Burke, approaches the definition of taste gingerly, worrying that to define it too exactly may ultimately circumscribe criticism. He concludes that the principles of taste, whatever they are, must be the same for all men:

> there is no difference in the manner of their being affected, nor in the causes of the affection; but in the *degree* there is a difference, which arises from two causes principally; either from a greater degree of natural sensibility, or from a closer and longer attention to the object.[15]

In this passage we may note the drive of the empiricist to reduce the problem of taste to one of measurement. The difference is that of greater or smaller, more or less. Unfortunately for the empiricist working in the area of the subjective, the subjective elements are, by Locke's definition, not the measurable ones. The measurable ones have already been designated as primary and objective qualities.

Like Hume, Burke is aware of these difficulties. When he comes to define "taste," he recognizes, first, that it is by no means a simple idea "but is partly made up of a perception of the primary pleasures of sense, of the secondary pleasures of the imagination, and of the conclusions of the reasoning faculty,

[14] Shaftesbury, *Characteristics of Men, Manners, Opinions, Times* (1711).
[15] Quotations from Burke are from *A Philosophical Inquiry into the Origin of Our Ideas of the Sublime and Beautiful* (1757).

concerning the various relations of these, and concerning the human passions, manners, and actions."

In these various efforts to establish objective standards in a welter of subjectivity, we discover the sources of such ideas as an isolable "aesthetic emotion" or "aesthetic state," the related idea of "aesthetic distance," and various distinctions between the beautiful and the simply agreeable. Hume remarks: "A perfect serenity of mind, a recollection of thought, a due attention to the object; if any of these circumstances be wanting, our experiment will be fallacious, and we shall be unable to judge of the catholic and universal beauty."

Until this state of mind can be theoretically separated from animalistic feelings of undifferentiated pleasure and pain, it cannot be particularly attractive as the ground of critical judgment. Immanuel Kant faces this problem and attempts an answer. He assumes that neither criticism nor any department of learning can proceed until it determines the object it is to examine. Art must be regarded as something with its own ends, which are not the ends of history, philosophy, science, morality, or theology. Kant supposes that there is a certain disinterest in our response to art. By disinterest Kant simply means that in our response to art we are not inhibited by utilitarian concerns. Art is purposive but paradoxically it exists without a purpose. The disinterest with which we view it makes it different from other objects: Kant's analysis is made in terms of the human response, not in terms of the object itself. But he contends there must be something in the nature of the object that makes our response what it is.

The idea of the beautiful, Kant says, is arrived at through disinterest: "Taste is the faculty of judging of an object or a method of representing it by an entirely *disinterested* satisfaction or dissatisfaction. The object of such satisfaction is called *beautiful*." [16] Apprehension of the beautiful is not, however, a cognitive process:

> since the person who judges feels himself quite *free* as regards the satisfaction which he attaches to the object, he cannot find the ground of this satisfaction in any private conditions connected with his own subject, and hence it must be regarded as grounded on what he can presuppose in every other person. Consequently he must believe that he has reason for attributing a similar satisfaction to everyone. He will therefore speak of the beautiful as if beauty were a characteristic of the object and the judgment

[16] Quotations from Kant are from *Critique of Judgment*, tr. by J. H. Bernard (New York: Hafner, 1956).

> logical (constituting a cognition of the object by means of concepts of it), although it is only aesthetical . . . .

One must distinguish between beauty and simple pleasure in the object by examining one's own response. Utilitarian motives must be eliminated in order to make the response aesthetic only, and not cognitive. Further, rules of beauty cannot be applied *a priori* or generally to a variety of objects. The result would be a cognitive or logical judgment of the object rather than an aesthetic one.

Kant goes deeper than Burke in examining the "pleasures of sense" and drawing distinctions between kinds of response. He attempts in a much more systematic way to face the problem Hume faced in his insistence on a sort of detachment or "perfect serenity of mind" before a work of art. The result is a distinction between the pleasurable or agreeable and the beautiful. Coleridge, deeply influenced by Kant and Friedrich von Schelling, borrows this distinction and simplifies it somewhat in *On the Principles of Genial Criticism Concerning the Fine Arts.* The word "agreeable" is used by us in two senses. The first usage describes that which is "congruous with the primary constitution of our senses." Certain colors, like green, are naturally agreeable to the eye. The second usage describes something that by force of habit has become agreeable to us—tobacco, for example.

The beautiful is different in kind from such experiences, and it can actually contain what is agreeable, disagreeable, or both: "The sense of beauty subsists in simultaneous intuition of the relation of parts, each to each, and of all to a whole: exciting an immediate and absolute complacency, without intervenence, therefore, of any interest, sensual, or intellectual."

This distinction looms very large in modern criticism, and there will be occasion to mention it again. Here it is important to notice that it represents an attempt to objectify artistic value in an age that threatened to reduce such value to simple subjective pleasure. It seeks to impose no arbitrary rules of value arrived at by generalization and logical schema. It implies that each artistic work generates its own principles of order. In all these discussions there is the implicit understanding that the term "pleasure" with its many meanings is too broad to be useful. More subtle distinctions are necessary to show varieties of favorable response to objects.

A second wave of concern with subjectivity occurs in the late nineteenth century in what is commonly called impressionistic criticism. The impressionistic critic, of whom Anatole France (1844–1924) is the exemplar, despairs of aesthetics, ignores the efforts of the eighteenth century to establish principles of taste, and in fact rejects the possibility of any science:

> Aesthetics is based upon nothing solid. It is a castle in the air. Some have sought to base it upon ethics. But there is no such thing as ethics. There is no such thing as sociology. Nor is there such a thing as biology. The completion of the sciences never existed save in the mind of M. Auguste Comte, whose work is a prophecy. When biology has been created, that is in a few million years' time, we shall perhaps be able to construct a sociology. It will be the work of a great many centuries; after which it will be permissible to create an aesthetic science on solid foundations.[17]

France suggests sarcastically that by the time such foundations have been built the sun will nearly have burned itself out. Meanwhile, the critic should be honest with himself and his readers. He should simply be "one who relates the adventures of his soul among masterpieces." Honesty requires that when the critic judges he should announce by way of preface, "Gentlemen, I am going to speak of myself on the subject of Shakespeare, or Racine, or Pascal, or Goethe."

Rather than accept this skepticism, this insistence that the mind is hopelessly enclosed in its own activities, critics have contrived complete escapes from the problem of the reader. Among many modern critics the whole affective approach to literature comes under severe attack, principally because the empirical problem seems impossible to solve. In a well-known essay entitled "The Affective Fallacy," W. K. Wimsatt and M. C. Beardsley hold that an approach to literature via its effects on the reader presents a special case of "epistemological skepticism" in which "the poem itself, as an object of specifically critical judgment, tends to disappear." [18] Without an object to discuss and evaluate as an object with its own special characteristics, one is forced back upon the "impressionism and relativism" of a variety of readers. The authors isolate two species of affective criticism for punishment, that of I. A. Richards, which they call the emotive form of this criticism, and that of Max Eastman, which they describe as the imaginative form.[19]

[17] From the preface to *Life and Letters,* fourth series, tr. by Bernard Miall (New York: Dodd, Mead, 1928).
[18] In W. K. Wimsatt, *The Verbal Icon* (Lexington: Univ. of Kentucky Press, 1954), pp. 21–39.
[19] See Max Eastman, *The Enjoyment of Poetry* (New York: Scribner's, 1951), and *The Literary Mind* (New York: Scribner's, 1932).

They recall that in *The Foundations of Aesthetics* (1948), Richards' collaboration with C. K. Ogden and James Wood, sixteen types of affective theory are outlined and one is adopted. This is the theory of "synaesthesis," or that in which beauty is described as "an equilibrium of appetencies" in the reader. This theory Richards tends to favor in actual critical practice. Although in his *Practical Criticism* he talks much about the response of various readers he has tested, he is primarily engaged in documenting what he considers misreadings or characteristic misjudgments and actually treats poems objectively as Kant says we must pretend to do. Richards cannot talk precisely enough about response without losing the poem, and he cannot talk about the poem without disregarding response or regarding it in a normative way.

Eastman's theory of imaginative vividness, Wimsatt and Beardsley point out, has many analogues. One of the best known is the critical test proposed by A. E. Housman (1859–1936): Recite a poem while shaving. If the bristles stand out, the poem is a success.[20] A similar attitude is present in remarks of praise seen often in reviews: "When you read this piece, you really believe you are there." One can easily see that such criticism cannot really establish precise relationships between the reader's responses and the qualities of the object that apparently cause them. Wimsatt and Beardsley point out that on the surface it may not seem to make much difference whether the critic talks in terms of the reader's response or in terms of the poem as an objective structure. They insist, however, that it actually makes all the difference. A critic who begins with the reader will remain to some extent isolated in the subjective. His criticism will probably be vague and without considerable regard for matters of form, of medium. Wimsatt and Beardsley opt for a discussion of the poem, not the reader:

> The more specific the account of the emotion induced by a poem, the more nearly it will be an account of the reasons for emotion, the poem itself, and the more reliable it will be as an account of what the poem is likely to induce in other—sufficiently informed—readers.

In two books, *Principles of Literary Criticism* (1928) and *Practical Criticism* (1929), Richards employed psychological language that attacked "the phantom aesthetic state," maintaining

---

[20] For Housman's criticism see *The Name and Nature of Poetry* (London: Cambridge Univ. Press, 1933).

that there is no isolable aesthetic experience. He argues that ever since Kant's attempt to describe aesthetic judgment as "disinterested, universal, unintellectual," the problem of artistic value has been hopelessly muddled:

> When we look at a picture, or read a poem, or listen to music, we are not doing something quite unlike what we were doing on our way to the Gallery or when we dressed in the morning. The fashion in which the experience is caused in us is different, and as a rule the experience is more complex and, if we are successful, more unified. But our activity is not of a fundamentally different kind.[21]

We shall see, however, that Richards allows the "perfect serenity of mind" of Hume and Kant's "disinterest" to creep back in a different form. If he does not do this, he will not be able to distinguish various sorts of pleasure and will find himself trapped in an undiscriminating hedonism. Richards' view is that "anything is valuable which will satisfy an appetency without involving the frustration of some equal or more *important* appetency." In everyday life we are constantly involved in situations in which more important appetencies are frustrated by lesser ones. Because in reading literature we are not involved in the matters that are described, we are able to achieve an equilibrium of impulses, a fully organized experience. The aesthetic state that Richards attacks as phantasmal reappears not as a special mental ability, but as mental balance. This view is not really very different from Kant's idea that art, having no utilitarian purposiveness, is conducive to aesthetic disinterest in the reader. Actually, however, Richards' position is not as subtle as either Hume's or Kant's; it is dogged by an unsophisticated behaviorist jargon. His own experiments with readers, reported in *Practical Criticism,* lead to discouraging conclusions. In that book he reports that he gave members of his Cambridge poetry classes thirteen poems to read without benefit of titles, authors, or relevant information of any kind. The students were to evaluate each poem. Many students could not make out the plain sense of several poems; many could not apprehend their sensuous qualities; many had great difficulty with imagery. Even more crucial for Richards' point of view was that most of the readers brought all sorts of irrelevant attitudes and feelings to the poems that corrupted their own responses. They exhibited sentimentality, inhibition, and doctrinal rigidity, and they reacted in stock ways to apparently

[21] Richards, *op. cit.,* pp. 16–17.

familiar situations. Finally, they exhibited naive preconceptions about poetic techniques and critical principles. All in all, it appears from *Practical Criticism* that readers are generally incapable of responding to poetry in the manner Richards describes in *Principles of Literary Criticism;* his students were either incapable of understanding the poems or unable to free themselves from the commitments of everyday life when they faced poems; thus the therapeutic function of balancing emotions, which Richards assigned to the experience of poetry, apparently could not occur. The students would have to be trained to read, mainly, he implies, to clear their minds of irrelevancies. What would the result of such training be? Perhaps it would be a different state of mind. The "phantom aesthetic state" is a persistent ghost.

More important, when Richards discusses the students' responses he implies that some of the poems are obviously better than others. In doing so, he seems to be turning to the poems as objective things and drawing critical principles from an examination of their structures, not from an examination of their readers, whose judgments have proved far too capricious. This has led Wimsatt and Beardsley to remark that Richards has actually contributed significantly to a more objective sort of criticism by insisting "1. that rhythm (the vague, if direct, expression of emotion) and poetic form in general are intimately connected with and interpreted by other and more precise parts of poetic meaning, 2. that poetic meaning is inclusive or multiple and hence sophisticated."

Richards turns ultimately to an idea of organic form similar to that of Coleridge. In fact, his later book, *Coleridge on Imagination,* quixotically attempts to convert Coleridge's thought into a behavioristic language. Although Richards apparently refuses to leap from the subject to the object, he surreptitiously invades the object, leaning in practice toward an objective criticism. His insistence on the therapeutic function of literature is difficult to sustain empirically. He cannot produce a patient who has been cured. Nor, for that matter, can he find the perfect reader to make an evaluation of the poem. If he could, of course, the reader would not *need* the therapy that the poem supposedly offers.

Others have tried to establish the therapeutic nature of literature with reference to psychoanalysis. Sigmund Freud (1856–1939) was not at all hesitant to point out that he did not discover the unconscious. That discovery, he said, had been made by the poets.

Freud was more interested in the writer's relation to the work than the reader's. His well-known discussion in *The Interpretation of Dreams* of the oedipal situation in *Hamlet* turns to an analysis of Shakespeare himself: "It can, of course, be only the poet's own psychology, with which we are confronted in *Hamlet*." Nevertheless, where Freud is writing about the psychology of the poet, as in "Creative Writers and Day-Dreaming," he is inclined to consider the audience as well:

> The unreality of the writer's imaginative world . . . has very important consequences for the technique of his art; for many things which, if they were real, could give no enjoyment, can do so in the play of phantasy, and many excitements which, in themselves, are actually distressing, can become a source of pleasure for the hearers and spectators at the performance of a writer's work.[22]

This appears to be a Freudian version of the phantom aesthetic state based on aesthetic distance.

At the conclusion of his essay, Freud speculates about the mystery of how the writer leads us to accept his offering:

> The writer softens the character of his egoistic day-dreams by altering and disguising it, and he bribes us by the purely formal —that is, aesthetic—yield of pleasure which he offers us in the presentation of his phantasies. We give the name of an *incentive bonus*, or a *forepleasure*, to a yield of pleasure such as this, which is offered to us so as to make possible the release of still greater pleasure arising from deeper psychical sources. In my opinion, all the aesthetic pleasure which a creative writer affords us has the character of a forepleasure of this kind, and our actual enjoyment of an imaginative work proceeds from a liberation of tensions in our minds. It may even be that not a little of this effect is due to the writer's enabling us thenceforward to enjoy our own day-dreams without self-reproach or shame.

Freud's attitudes toward the poet are finally, I think, as ambivalent as Plato's. On the one hand, he speaks with great admiration of poets and recognizes that his own psychoanalytical studies owe much to them. On the other, he thinks of art as a "narcotic" with the derogatory implications this word carries, particularly

---

[22] Sigmund Freud, "Creative Writers and Day-Dreaming" in James Strachey, ed., *The Complete Psychological Works*, Vol. IX, tr. by I. F. Duff (London: Hogarth Press, 1959).

in the vocabulary of someone of highly materialistic persuasion. For Freud, art is perhaps ultimately harmless, but nevertheless it is illusory, and there is something neurotic about creating illusions. They remind Freud, no doubt, of the phantasies of his patients. Philosophically, Freud's location of reality is very naive. He talks about a principle of reality, but he does not explore the problem of where reality is.

Yet for Freud art does have functions. In his very illuminating essay "Freud and Literature," Lionel Trilling enumerates them:

> it has a therapeutic effect in releasing mental tension; it serves the cultural purpose of acting as a "substitute gratification" to reconcile men to the sacrifices they have made for culture's sake; it promotes the social sharing of highly valued emotional experiences; and it recalls men to their cultural ideals. This is not everything that some of us would find that art does, yet even this is a good deal for a "narcotic" to do.[23]

Yet there is nothing in this analysis that enables us to separate art from other things performing these functions. Perhaps this is because Freud pays no attention to the medium. The analogy between dreams and art reaches its limit at this point. The artist, awake and conscious, employs a medium. Once the medium is introduced as of critical importance, problems of imitation flood back in, and the relation of the reader to the medium must be considered.

The study of dreams has been related to the anthropological study of myths and rituals, and this relationship has been of interest to literary critics. The critics are particularly in the debt of James G. Frazer (1854–1941), author of *The Golden Bough*; various members of the Cambridge school of anthropology; Bronislaw Malinowski (1884–1942), who studied the primitive life of the Trobriand Islanders; and Ernst Cassirer, the anthropological philosopher. It has been recognized that literary conventions have some relation to certain conventions of primitive consciousness. Primitive man thinks by metaphor and analogy. Metaphorical fitness is as important as, and in many situations vastly more important than, utilitarian logic. He does not make the rigid distinctions that civilized man makes, or seeks to make, between thought and feeling. He jealously guards his methaphoric sense of the unity of life against the divisive analytic tendencies of the intellect. Some modern critics suggest that literature and the other arts provide a way of ordering experience that

[23] Trilling, *op. cit.*, p. 54.

is dialectically opposed to that of reason and that works toward unity in metaphor rather than multiplicity in analysis. They have held that this tendency, if suppressed in the individual or the society in favor of the domination of analytics, results in disruption of the psychic life. According to this view, we are all partly primitive, and necessarily so. It implies that there is a demand in human beings for unification with objects in nature other than the self and that this can be effected through renewal of a mythic attitude toward metaphor. Let us take as an example a savage who lives on the banks of the Nile and holds quite seriously that he and his tribesmen are crocodiles. This does not mean that he allows his metaphor to invade completely his practical life. He is not about to jump into the river and swim about with the crocodiles. But he establishes through the hypostasis of language a *relation* to other things. He acts upon what Martin Buber insists that man requires: a sense of the *thou*-ness rather than the *it*-ness of his surroundings, whether these surroundings are people, animals, trees, or stones.

If this view has accuracy, it shows that modern education is far too heavily weighted toward the analytical and the abstract. Elements of ancient myths—particularly the principle of animism, the collapse of measurement in favor of metonymy, and the projection of subjective space and time—are formal characteristics of literature that oppose our analytic tendencies. If one holds that literary structures perform a function necessary to biological man by reasserting a relation to objects, by getting across the subject-object gap, then one is holding not for a balancing of appetencies, as in Richards, but for a sort of dialectic of opposing forces. These forces have in the past been loosely called the rational and the irrational, the understanding and the imagination, the drive toward analysis and the drive toward synthesis. It follows that our educations should lead to a prolific contrariety of art and analysis in our lives. In this view, art becomes didactic, not because it teaches us concepts, but because it *presents* a unified world to us, and in this sense it is perhaps intellectually therapeutic *and* delightful.

# 4 POSSESSION AND EXPRESSION

Consideration of the poem as being closely related to the poet, indeed as an expression of the poet's being, is comparatively recent in the history of criticism. For centuries the poet was depicted, sometimes seriously and sometimes not so seriously, as someone who was possessed by the Muse. At the beginning of the *Odyssey* Homer does not merely ask for aid from the divine Muse, he gives himself up to her. He invites her to begin the tale as she wishes. Homer considers himself a sort of vessel—in Aristotelian terms an efficient cause—through which greater spirits speak. There is sanction, then, for Plato's argument, pursued so relentlessly at Ion's expense, that the poet is simply not responsible for his utterances:

> For all good poets, epic as well as lyric, compose their beautiful poems not by art, but because they are inspired and possessed. And as the Corybantian revellers when they dance are not in their right mind, so the lyric poets are not in their right mind when they are composing their beautiful strains: but when falling under the power of music and metre they are inspired and possessed; like Bacchic maidens who draw milk and honey from the rivers when they are under the influence of Dionysus but not when they are in their right mind. And the soul of the lyric poet does the same, as they themselves say; for they tell us that they bring songs from honeyed fountains, culling them out of the gardens and dells of the Muses; they, like the bees, winging their way from flower to flower. And this is true. For the poet is a light and winged and holy thing, and there is no invention in him until he has been inspired and is out of his senses . . . .[1]

[1] Quotations from Plato are from the translation by Benjamin Jowett in his *The Dialogues of Plato,* 4th ed. (Oxford, Eng.: Clarendon Press, 1953).

As we have seen, Plato finds this condition awe-inspiring but dangerous to the commonwealth. He employs the already venerable idea of possession by the Muse as support for his decree banishing the poet from his Republic. If we follow logically the idea of possession, we recognize that the poet cannot be held accountable for his creations because they are not really *his* creations. Possibly because of the tradition of possession by the Muse, the ancients were not very interested in the relation of the poet to his work. This may be difficult for some of us to understand because we are so strongly influenced by a critical tradition emphasizing above everything else the poet's presence in the work or the work as an emanation of the poet's feelings. Yet this tradition did not flower until early in the nineteenth century with the so-called Romantic movement.

From Aristotle's time and perhaps before, there was plenty of discussion about how to write poems, plenty of advice to the poet, but little interest in the poem as an expression of the poet's soul. In his definition of tragedy, Aristotle concerns himself with tragedy as an imitation. He desires to show what constitutes a good tragedy, and he approaches this problem by discussing mainly the structure of plot and subsidiary elements. He does not suggest that the poet's nature helps define tragedy, nor does he suggest that any critical principles can be derived from the relation of the poet to his work.

The same holds true of Horace. His advice to the poet is totally impersonal: Stick with tradition when possible, avoid extremes, work hard. Horace believes that a good poet must be a gentleman, but he goes no deeper into the question of the poet's nature. His criticism is really directed toward the relation of the poem to an audience.

The tradition of possession by the Muse has managed to persist into our own era. Robert Graves has defined the function of poetry as "religious invocation of the Muse" and has insisted that the Muse has been known to invade poets who have eaten certain mushrooms. Less seriously, or perhaps more cynically, A. E. Housman gave Muse-like power to the quaffing of a pint of beer followed by a long walk. For Kathleen Raine, more solemn, inspiration may arrive in any number of natural forms—bird, leaf, daybreak, moth, or flower. Most serious are those who hold the Bible to be the product of a divine inspiration flowing forth through the minds and pens of its composers and, of course, its translators. It is interesting that in motion pictures—to some extent a barometer of our sentimentalities—artists and writers are most often depicted as possessed. The frenzied composer or painter is a stock figure in the movie trade. It is perhaps just as well. Cornel Wilde playing Chopin needs all the help the Muse can muster. In any case, veteran moviegoers are by now inured to the sight of the painter furiously spattering paint, the pianist pounding the keyboard (Jimmy Durante's routine is perhaps a parody of possession), the composer (inevitably a Romantic, incidentally) scribbling furiously, affected visibly by the din of celestial chords.

These modern versions of possession have a certain uniqueness. It is as if the possession is generated from within and whatever is there must be expelled. In the movies, piano-pounding and paper-rending are apparently cathartic—for the artist if not for the audience. There is also something more individualistic about the whole matter than possession traditionally implies. Indeed, in modern versions, possession recedes to a considerable extent, and self-expression takes its place. The poet may be driven by inner forces he cannot fully control, but he knows what he is doing. William Blake's remarks about his prophetic books reflect a little of both attitudes. He emphasized possession in a letter to Thomas Butts in 1803:

> I have in these three years composed an immense number of verses on One Grand Theme, Similar to Homer's Iliad or Milton's Paradise Lost, the Persons and Machinery intirely new to the Inhabitants of Earth (some of the Persons Excepted). I have written this poem from immediate Dictation, twelve or sometimes twenty or thirty lines at a time, without Premeditation & even against my Will, the Time it has taken in writing was thus render'd Non Existent, & an immense Poem Exists which seems to be the Labour of a long Life, all produc'd without Labour or Study.

It is not easy to decide how this should be taken. Blake's way of talking was hyperbolic, and he liked to emphasize the difference between imaginative acts and those of the reason. He is writing here to a patron, whom he wishes to impress; perhaps he wishes to inspire awe. In his preface to *Jerusalem* he again mentions dictation, but one can interpret the last sentence to mean that he consciously made certain decisions:

> When this Verse was first dictated to me I consider'd a Monotonous Cadence, like that used by Milton and Shakespeare & all writers of English Blank Verse, derived from the modern bondage of Rhyming, to be a necessary and indispensible part of verse. But I soon found that in the mouth of a true Orator such

monotony was not only awkward, but as much a bondage as rhyme itself. I therefore have produced a variety in every line, both of cadences & number of syllables. Every word and every letter is studied and put into its fit place.

The coexistence of dictation and studied composition is not easy to imagine without also imagining some curious division of labor, the spirits providing the matter and Blake the technique. It is not easy, however, to imagine Blake himself accepting such a separation between form and content. Indeed, he vigorously objects to such a separation. The answer to the problem lies, I think, in where Blake locates the dictating spirit. For Blake, God does not exist up in the sky or beyond man but within him, expressing Himself in each individual and as that individual. Possession or dictation is therefore for Blake the exercise of the imagination unfettered by the demands of the reason, the false god who seeks to impose his will from without. Blake was dissociating himself not only from the narrow rationalism of his times but also from tendencies to describe poetic creation in mechanistic terms. But there is perhaps something unconscious and robotlike in the role of the poet implied by the Muse. If in *Jerusalem* the Muse dictates to Blake, it insists that he report his own imaginative experiences, for the poem is in one sense about writing a poem with Blake its hero.

By Blake's time, invocation to the Muse had become rather a bore, mainly because it had been overworked and reduced to a device, but also because the idea of possession had given way to the idea of self-expression. In *Don Juan* Lord Byron (1788–1824) actually jokes at the Muse's expense. He refers to *his* Muse; he indicates that by comparison to Southey's, *his* Muse is "pedestrian." In Canto Two his "sober muse" is powerless to prevent his digressions. He begins Canto Three with the ultimate insult: "Hail, Muse! *et cetera.*—We left Juan sleeping." With this device he asserts that he will do what he pleases with his poem, which is mainly to express himself. Among Romantic critics what is generally to be expressed is not a series of rational truths but sincere feelings. The best known Romantic statement illustrating this is William Wordsworth's assertion that poetry is "the spontaneous overflow of powerful feelings."

With this emphasis upon self-expression, we see the Aristotelian idea of purgation turned around so that it no longer refers to a therapeutic effect upon the audience but to the purgation of the poet's passions. If the poet has certain feelings inside him, the poetic act is to expel them in poetic form. This theme of purgation is dominant in Byron, important in Keats, and apparent in the poetry of Romanticism generally. In his excellent study of Romantic expressivism, M. H. Abrams has shown how Romantic theorists, pursuing their interest in the artist's relation to his work, concern themselves with the poet's own catharsis:[2] Among these theorists William Hazlitt (1778–1830) anticipated Sigmund Freud with a theory of wish-fulfillment and discussed Alexander Pope as compensating for his deformity by writing poems.[3] Another thinker of particular interest is John Keble (1792–1886), who wrote: "Poetry is the indirect expression in words, most appropriately in metrical words, of some overpowering emotion, or ruling taste, or feeling, the direct indulgence whereof is somehow repressed." [4]

For Keble poetry is a catharsis for the poet and an objectification of his ungratified desires. Keble's further explanation that these desires are often disguised points toward more recent attempts of psychoanalytical critics to examine just such desires, to move from the work back into the poet's mind, in short to think the poem important as a means to enter that mind. In these developments the Muse seems to be revived as a power working mysteriously below the threshold of consciousness. With Freud the Muse receives a new name and location. To some extent, however, the Muse is no longer an artist—at least in the sense that "artificer" conveys.

The development of scientific method carried implications that led ultimately to the emergence of the expressive theory of art and its emphasis upon the artist's mental activity. From the strictly empirical point of view, only that which is measurable is objective, and only the objective is the real. John Locke's distinction between primary and secondary qualities of experience formalizes this view, for Locke's distinction is really between the measurable and unmeasurable. For example, light can be measured, but certain qualities inherent in the experience of light cannot. These qualities—the so-called secondary ones —are ignored in measurement. If one locates reality in the measurable and if one insists on making poetry deal with reality, then one must begin to consider most of the conventions of poetry simply as ornaments hung on to empirical statements and

[2] M. H. Abrams, *The Mirror and the Lamp: Romantic Theory and the Critical Tradition* (New York: Norton, 1958), pp. 138–48.
[3] See Hazlitt's essays "On Dreams" and "On Poetry in General."
[4] John Keble, Review of Lockhart's *Life of Scott* in *Occasional Papers and Reviews* (1877), p. 6.

poetry itself, perhaps, as an ornament hung on to life. Synecdoche, for example, would have to be recognized as an example of a serious breach of logic, because a part cannot be the whole and conform to the measurable standards of reality. This view implies a naive idea of the relation of language to the reality it is supposed to describe.

There are other possible results. One is insistence that the poet's discourse conform to the empirical facts. Thomas Hobbes' opinion verges upon this view. Although he holds that the subject of poetry is "the manners of men, not natural causes; manners presented, not dictated; and manners feigned . . ." he insists: "Beyond the actual works of nature a Poet may now go; but beyond the conceived possibility of nature, never." Hobbes (1588–1679) does not go to the extreme in this matter, but it is possible to see in his "Answer to Davenant's 'Preface' to *Gondibert*" (1650) the embryo of an idea of naive imitation that could disregard all the efforts of previous critics to protect the poet's freedom of invention. Mainly, the theory would subordinate art to science.

There is no question that this frame of mind leads to a consideration of poetry simply as prettified discourse. In this view poetry would turn to the verse essay (as it partly did for a time) and to scientific exposition such as that absurdly represented by these lines from Erasmus Darwin's "The Economy of Vegetation":

> Hence orient Nitre owes its sparkling birth,
> And with prismatic crystals gems the earth,
> O'er tottering domes the filmy foliage crawls,
> Or frosts with branching plumes the mould'ring walls;
> As woos Azotic Gas the virgin Air,
> And veils in crimson clouds the yielding fair.

The tendency in eighteenth-century poetry to employ poetic devices merely as decoration repelled Wordsworth and induced him to make his now well-known statement against "the gaudiness and inane phraseology of many modern writers" and those who "indulge in arbitrary and capricious habits of expression." He wrote in 1800 of his own *Lyrical Ballads*: "personifications of abstract ideas rarely occur in these volumes; and are utterly rejected, as an ordinary device to elevate the style, and raise it above prose." There lurks here Goethe's distinction between allegory and symbolism. Wordsworth rejects the poet who begins with an abstract idea, invents an indirect or allegorical representation of it, and then implicitly invites us to translate it back to its true meaning. Allegory so viewed appears to be a form of decoration and poetry merely decorated information presented in the form of generalization from empirical data. Wordsworth had a broader idea of the function of poetic language and believed that poetry conveys truth "not standing upon external testimony, but carried alive into the heart by passion."

It is unfortunate that his own language immediately preceding these words is misleading: "Aristotle, I have been told, has said, that Poetry is the most philosophic of all writing: it is so: its object is truth, not individual and local, but general, and operative . . . ." Wordsworth, like Samuel Johnson in his famous statement about the streaks of the tulip, either does not understand that the "general" is the result of empirical, scientific method, or is using language without precision. To assume that poetry is general is to make the poet simply a decorator of scientific generalizations. It is more important for Wordsworth to get this straight than for Johnson, because his attitude, fully observed, clearly insists on the individual soul and its unique experiences and expressiveness as the wellspring of poetry. Luckily, Wordsworth rights himself at once, speaking of "truth which is its own testimony."

Without rejecting Locke's distinction, some critics found an alternative to considering poetry merely as decorated discourse. This was to argue that although science had captured objectivity, subjectivity was the realm of the poet. Abrams illustrates the idea with the lines from Wordsworth's "Tintern Abbey" describing the act of perception as that in which the mind half creates and half perceives. In a note to this poem, Wordsworth refers to a passage from Edward Young's *Night Thoughts,* in which Young (1683–1765) describes how our subjective experience gives "taste to fruits; and harmony to groves." Abrams remarks:

> In Locke's dualism . . . we have the view that our perception of the sensible world consists partly of elements reflecting things as they are, and partly of elements which are merely "ideas of the mind" without "likeness of something existing without." Locke, therefore, implicitly gave the mind a partnership in sense perception; what Young did was to convert this into an active partnership of "giving," "making," and "creation." In this simple metaphoric substitution we find Locke's sensationalism in the process

of converting itself into what is often considered its epistemo-logical opposite.[5]

Locke is usually interpreted as emphasizing the reality of the primary qualities and the unreality of the subjective secondary ones. Wordsworth is interested in the passage from Young because Young implicitly congratulates the mind on its creative powers and its partnership in making reality, which for him is a combination or partnership of objective and subjective experience.

A possible result of making subjectivity the realm of the poet is to reduce the art of poetry to a cry of pure emotion, to purge from its language anything but expressions of feeling. Such a view seems to be reflected in the composition of some of Edgar Allan Poe's poems. The poet seems to have become imprisoned in his own subjectivity. His creations are to be considered merely as fantasies. The world remains bifurcated into that understood by science, rationality, and empiricism on the one hand and that imagined by art, feeling, and subjectivity on the other. The epistemology of George Berkeley helps to establish the essential issues here, because he entirely reverses Locke. He accuses not the subjectivist but the objectivist of indulging in fantasy; he holds that if we are to be truly empirical we must admit that we can know only our perceptions and that they give us only the subjective, unmeasurable qualities. The primary qualities are inferred from them. In Locke the objective dominates. In Young objective and subjective keep their places, separate but equal. In Berkeley, the subjective dominates. Although Berkeley makes a cogent criticism of the abstract unreality of the primary world, he nevertheless seems in the eyes of some of his interpreters to isolate each individual hopelessly in his own perceptions.

Certainly a central awareness of Romantic poetry is the isolation of the individual within his own feelings and perceptions. Generally, however, Romantic criticism struggles against isolation. It rejects naive realism and goes beyond the separate equality of subject and object implied in the passage from Young. It wishes to distinguish literature from scientific modes of thought. Because science implies a distinction between subject and object, it tends, rather than taking the subjective side, to insist on the artificiality of the distinction itself, although it proceeds from a position based firmly in the perceiving mind.

[5] Abrams, *op. cit.*, p. 63.

It places art and the unification of experience on one side and on the other science, analytics, and the bifurcation of experience into subject and object. In the *Biographia Literaria,* Coleridge makes a characteristic point:

> During the act of knowledge itself, the objective and subjective are so instantly united, that we cannot determine to which of the two priority belongs. There is here no first, and no second; both are coinstantaneous and one. While I am attempting to explain this intimate coalition, I must suppose it dissolved. I must necessarily set out from the one, to which I therefore give hypothetical antecedence, in order to arrive at the other.

It is not a great distance from what Coleridge says here to the idea that there is something in our rationalistic use of language that impels us to talk in terms of subject and object, implying a division where really there is none. In order to proceed toward an adequate statement of the situation, we must begin at one linguistic pole and progress from it toward a more acceptable formulation. Coleridge sets out in just this way, choosing to move from the subjective to the objective. In this choice he is strongly influenced by Kant and Schelling. It is the Kantian Coleridge with whom I am concerned here. Immanuel Kant attempts to overcome the subject-object distinction by proceeding from mind to nature. The mind operates in the forms of time and space, which are subjective in that we think and perceive in these terms but objective in that they are the spectacles none of us can remove. From this premise Kant deduces the categories of understanding—quantity, quality, relation, modality —which are the laws by which the mind works. Working upon the manifold of sensation through these categories, the mind constructs reality. It is true that things exist in themselves independent of us, but we cannot ever know anything directly about them. We can only know our ideas of them, the fictions of objectivity we create that constitute and explain things.

It is important here to note two things: First, this view implies that the mind is creative even of nature scientifically described, and second, there was never any doubt that poetic fictions were creations of the mind of the poet, except among those who took the idea of possession literally. With objective nature reduced to mental creation, it was possible to consider artistic fictions as perhaps in their own way just as significant as objective fictions. To put it another way, if the mind constructs its reality, or all the reality it can know, then *all* the activities of the mind take on a new importance. We make distinctions among the kinds of activities it engages in or the kinds of creations it effects. The activity of the mind as an art-producing thing demands exploration.

Although empiricism consistently emphasized objectivity, its tendency as far back as Descartes was to begin with the mind and from there to deduce a primary reality. It contributed to a theory that ultimately called in question the reality of the very same objectivity it sought to establish. As a result, it again turned interest to the creative process, but to creativity considered in a broader perspective.

Poets, as Freud pointed out, had always been interested in the mind, but the Romantic interest in it was more self-conscious than ever before, principally for those reasons already discussed. Because of emphasis upon the creativity of the mind and curiosity about it, criticism began to think of the poem as essentially an expression of the poet, as intimately related to his mind. It is interesting to see that neither Coleridge nor Wordsworth can discuss the idea of poetry without looking behind the poem to its author. The poem is definable for them only in terms of the poet's activity.

Wordsworth, speaking of poetry, must quickly turn from the poem to remark: "Taking up the subject, then, upon general grounds, let me ask, what is meant by the word Poet? What is a Poet?" He assures us that the poet is "a man speaking to men" (all else would smack of solipsism, one supposes), but he is more concerned with the poet's nature:

> a man, it is true, endowed with more lively sensibility, more enthusiasm and tenderness, who has a greater knowledge of human nature, and a more comprehensive soul, than are supposed to be common among mankind; a man pleased with his own passions and volitions, and who rejoices more than other men in the spirit of life that is in him; delighting to contemplate similar volitions and passions as manifested in the goings-on of the Universe, and habitually compelled to create them where he does not find them.

The passage suggests that the poet is a unifying force, joining nature and man, object and subject, transcending by means of the feelings a separation brought about by rationality. Wordsworth locates feeling not just in man but "in the goings-on of the Universe." This is possible because once the distinction between subject and object is destroyed, the feelings, previously locked in the subject by the principles of empiricism, can flow forth enveloping, framing, or forming nature; nature becomes a product of the total mental life, which includes feeling. Perhaps this interpretation makes Wordsworth more consistent than he really was when he made the remarks above, but the view is certainly implied in his language.

In the *Biographia Literaria,* Coleridge attempts to lay a theoretical groundwork before moving to his criticism of Wordsworth's poetry. But he does not define the word "poem." Instead, he retreats from the poem to invade the poet's mind and reach a definition of the word "imagination." The "primary imagination," he says, is a repetition in the finite mind of the eternal act of creation in the infinite I AM." In other words, the individual mind repeats in its perception the eternal act of God in creating the world. The "fancy" and the "secondary imagination" both proceed from this initial creativity, yet they are contrasted to each other. The fancy operates according to scientific method upon nature, after the secondary qualities of experience have been rationalistically removed. Art is a product of the secondary imagination that performs conscious acts: It "dissolves, diffuses, dissipates, in order to recreate; or where this process is rendered impossible, yet still at all events it struggles to idealize and unify." Coleridge calls this imaginative power "essentially vital," while the fancy, he implies, creates a world of inanimate or dead objects. It may be said that for Coleridge the secondary imagination is an animating principle similar to that which Wordsworth seems to posit when he attributes feelings to nature; the fancy is the opposite, purging consciousness from objects. This view reaffirms, incidentally, the organic use of the many conventions of poetry that are reduced to decoration in those theories that separate form and content. Animism becomes a sort of basic principle rather than a simple device. The world is alive because it is invested with life by a living mind.

As Abrams has pointed out, the central metaphor for a poem in Romantic critical theory is the organism.[6] Emphasis upon life, creativity, and process is implied in it, and it locates the poem in the process of its creation; thus it turns us effectively toward the poet himself. That Coleridge begins with a definition of the imagination indicates that he is probably more interested in the activity of poetic creation than in the poem as a completed object. But perhaps it is best to say that he is interested in the poem as a product of imaginative activity. The danger of this interest to a lesser critic than Coleridge might be formidable. It

[6] *Ibid.,* pp. 156–225.

could easily lead to disregard for the medium or to artificial separation of form and content. Coleridge's own theory can perhaps avert this danger. The analogy between the poem as the poet's creative act and the world as God's implies that the poem's principle of order is as unique as that of the world. Each poem generates its own order. Coleridge's organicism implies not a series of rules applied to a poem from without to which it should conform, but an order unique to itself that can only be discovered in the poem and is not applicable to any other poem. The poem is its own universe. To seek the principle of order in each poem is finally perhaps to retreat from the poet-poem relationship (only, of course, after establishing this principle, which attention to the relationship brought about) and view the poem as an objective thing. In this way the expressive theory of art prepares the way for its own metamorphosis into an objective theory, the subject of Chapter 5.

In summary, a criticism emphasizing the poet's relation to the poem arose along with an epistemology that divided experience into subjective and objective. This epistemology and the criticism related to it tended to attribute logic and reason to empirical and scientific method, which was analytical and divisive. Art was relegated to the realm of subjectivity and associated with those mental processes that were left—feeling, emotion, and so forth. Science and art were gradually distinguished as separate activities of the mind. Attitudes toward art as decorated rationality were followed by theories of art as pure expression of pure feeling. But since there were difficulties in empirically proving the existence of objectivity and since poets were unwilling to accept isolation within subjectivity, criticism was never content with a crude, emotive form of expressivism. The argument that the poem does no more than express something may easily turn into a theory of naive imitation, the object imitated being the feelings. It became necessary, in order to escape this problem, to insist that poetry was more or other than the expression of feeling. Helped along by new epistemological considerations, a mode of criticism developed that insisted that poetry was the product of the constitutive power of the mind, which, by expressing itself and its acts, helps to create what reality we can know.

It is now necessary to examine some of the implications for criticism of the emphasis upon the relation of poem to poet. We have seen that the idea of the poem as an expression of the poet's *feelings* was intimately associated with this emphasis from the beginning, so it is proper to use the remarks of Wordsworth on this matter as an introduction. The pronouncements below are all from his preface to the second edition of *Lyrical Ballads* (1800):

1. "For all good poetry is the spontaneous overflow of powerful feelings."
2. "Another circumstance must be mentioned which distinguishes these poems from the popular poetry of the day; it is this, that the feeling therein developed gives importance to the action and situation, and not the action and situation to the feeling."
3. "I have said that poetry is the spontaneous overflow of powerful feelings: it takes its origin from emotion recollected in tranquillity: the emotion is contemplated till, by a species of reaction, the tranquillity disappears, and an emotion, kindred to that which was before the subject of contemplation, is gradually produced, and does itself actually exist in the mind."

These remarks, taken from different parts of the preface but reproduced here in the order of their appearance, show Wordsworth gradually qualifying his initial statement. The first one, torn from context, is extreme. It seems to imply, through omission, that poetry consists of the feelings of the poet as they flow forth in the actual moment of high emotion. This would put a premium on the worst aspects of bad Romantic poetry— excess of interjection, a plethora of swooning, sighing, tears, and assorted cries, as well as a sort of automatic or spontaneous composition.

We see from number 2, however, that Wordsworth does not imagine the perfect poem to be merely spiritual ejaculation. He apparently wishes to remind the reader that a poem has action and situation—a structure. The feelings have a medium, even though the medium is there for the sake of the feelings. This notion causes us to reconsider number 1, and it leads to number 3, a new formulation that allows that time and the proper temper are necessary for objectification to occur. In any case, the poem does not and indeed must not come rushing forth at the very moment of the experience. It is important to note, however, that Wordsworth assumes the experience to be the poet's and no one else's.

The perspicuity of Wordsworth should not be underestimated here. His view not only has a great deal of originality; it also is more sophisticated than that of many others who did not anticipate the major difficulties in the popular emphasis, first, upon the poet, and, second, upon his feelings. Let us examine some implications of less sophisticated expressivism.

1. *If we take Wordsworth's first pronouncement alone, interesting difficulties occur.* "Overflow," implying a fountain or flood, suggests formlessness. "Spontaneous" supports the suggestion. The invitation, as we have seen, is to forgo attention to convention, to plot, even to words. The structure of the work must somehow be the structure of the feeling, whatever that is. But poems are made of words. Are feelings? Simply disregarded is the Aristotelian idea that the convergence of nature *with* a foreign medium is essential to poetic composition.

More than one Romantic critic has disregarded the medium, at least as it had been traditionally conceived. Previous to the development of the expressive point of view, the archetypical literary genre tended to be the epic. With the Romantics it came to be the lyric, for the lyric seemed superficially nearest to a spontaneous fountainlike expression of emotion. For Edgar Allan Poe (1809–49) the long poem was "simply a flat contradiction in terms." Though Poe looks at things in his essay "The Poetic Principle" from what he conceives to be the reader's point of view, it is clear he believes that not only the reader will be bored but that the author will be unable to sustain his power of expression throughout a long poem. This sort of attitude seems to have been prevalent even among poets who would not have admitted to it. For example, John Keats, who claimed that "the excellence of every art is its intensity," and "if Poetry comes not as naturally as the Leaves to a tree it had better not come at all," attempted but was not able to complete a major long poem.[7] Coleridge notoriously left *Christabel* unfinished and made the "unfinished" long poem "Kubla Khan" into a finished short poem about failure to complete a long one. Wordsworth's projected long poem was never finished. Byron's *Don Juan* breaks off uncompleted at his death. The theory of expression requires some new idea of poetic structure if the theory can overcome Poe's argument and manage to allow the long poem to exist at all. But unfortunately, as long as the expressive theory is naively imitative, its logical result for a long poem would be a poem the last line of which would be written as the poet expires. The structure of the poem would be based

---

[7] See letters to George and Thomas Keats, December 22, 1818, and to John Taylor, February 27, 1818.

upon an imitation of the temporal movement of the poet's feelings or a continuous expression of the poet's self from birth to death. One can see Byron playing with this issue in *Don Juan,* perhaps in his threat to write fifty cantos.

A related tendency of some criticism to value the apparently spontaneous or the fragment that causes transport is apparent in Matthew Arnold's concept of "touchstones," discrete passages of high feeling rather than whole poems.[8] If we extend these views only a little, we see the shape of an action as somehow getting in the emotion's way, or at the least we see a distinction developing between the poem and the poetical. Even Coleridge despite his organicism seems to have been affected by this when he remarked that "a poem of any length neither can be, or ought to be, all poetry." Vestiges of this attitude remain today.

For a different reason, but a related one, E. M. Forster remarks in *Aspects of the Novel*: "Yes—oh, dear, yes—the novel tells a story." Forster is actually attacking the emphasis upon realism at the expense of other sorts of formal principles. Curiously, Romantic criticism did presage, though often at the expense of form, a broader view of possible modes of unity and order in literary works. It became no longer necessary to treat the story line as the fundamental principle of order. Romantic expressivism paved the way for the so-called lyrical novel. It is doubtful that Forster's position could have been taken without the previous intervention of the expressive theory of art.

In this whole matter the example of Byron is an interesting one. Byron's cavalier treatment of the story line in *Don Juan* is a strategy to protect his own self-expression and have his plot at the same time. The main element of the poem is the poet expressing himself. The real action is Byron writing his poem. The apparent plot is the story of *Don Juan,* which Byron as the hero of his poem manipulates as if it were a Punch and Judy show. Of course, Byron's activity as Byron in the poem is not a spontaneous eruption from his mind; it is only made to appear so.

Theories of "spontaneous overflow" inevitably run up against several problems. First, they can give no attention to poetic form or the medium, which inevitably must be considered as enemies to the purity of the original intention. Second, little or no room is usually allowed for the intellect in poetic composition. This rejection of the intellect goes back to the split

---

[8] See "The Study of Poetry" (1880).

between subject and object, the subsequent split between feeling and thought grafted onto it, and the assignment of only feeling to poetry. Objective criticism eventually attempted to state the difference between poetry and other forms of discourse in another way, so that the poem was not assigned only the irrational feelings. The strategy was to reach a definition of the poem not in terms of mental powers but in terms of how it used language.

2. *If pure expression of the feelings or of the self is the poet's aim, the criterion of success is probably whether the poem is sincere.* Sincerity in such a situation is parallel to verisimilitude in a theory emphasizing imitation. If the author is alive, we can, I suppose, ask him whether he was expressing sincere feelings in any given poem—if we dare. But how are we to tell whether his answer is sincere? We are caught in an infinite regress. If the author is dead, even exhumation will not help. Lacking documents in the coffin, we are thrust back upon the only source of proof—the poem itself.

The criterion of sincerity raises another problem. Supposing it is possible to demonstrate that a poem is sincere, is that really an adequate criterion of its success after all? Will the feelings of a dull mind sincerely expressed be of the same value as the sincere feelings of a more profound mind? To put it more sharply, would a sincere poem by Edgar Guest be superior to an insincere one by his less popular contemporary, T. S. Eliot? Or, to go even farther, is it really possible for *any* poem to be insincere?

Sincerity need not refer to specific poems and, when used in literary talk, frequently does not. The poet's dedication to his art, much emphasized in the nineteenth century, can be described as a form of sincerity. Often, talk of dedication simply reflects an effort by artist and critic to explain a work's unpopularity with the public. The artist is seen by the critic or sees himself as working toward some vision or ideal, not toward delighting or teaching or curing. Related to this attitude is the expressive theory's own revival of the Muse. The Muse no longer necessarily invades the poet. In Robert Graves' version the poet writes his poems *to* the Muse, thereby asserting his freedom from public pressure and maintaining his dedicated self-expression.

3. *Can one really know what one is expressing?* With the development of depth psychology the matter of self-expression becomes more complicated, simply because it is now understood that the self is more complicated than most of us had thought.

The poet cannot be asked whether he has accurately and sincerely expressed himself because he probably does not know what he has unconsciously expressed. Modern poets notoriously refuse to comment upon their works, partly for this reason and partly also for reasons that will appear in Chapter 5. There is an additional complication: If the poet consciously expresses his feelings with sincerity but is unconsciously suppressing something, is he sincere or insincere? Unconscious material can hardly be amenable to a judgment of sincerity. Viewed as unconscious expression, poetry is unconsciously allegorical. The interpreter must act as the analyst. It is almost as if the Muse had reappeared in the form of the Freudian Id and the poet were again as helpless as Plato insisted he was.

4. *Under the expressive theory certain kinds of information external to the poem become useful.* The most important of these are the other works of the author and all that falls under biographical material. It would not have been at all clear to Aristotle that Sophocles' laundry lists might have some critical use, but T. S. Eliot was impelled to admit that Shakespeare's conceivably could have. The Romantic period ushered in the age of literary biography, and a literary scholarship grew up, centered upon all remnants of the author's life and works. That we know so little about Shakespeare is not because "Shakespeare" was a pseudonym for Francis Bacon or Edward de Vere. It is to some extent the result of pre-Romantic criticism's relative lack of interest in the author. Of course, biographies of famous writers existed previous to the nineteenth century, but, as an example, Walton wrote his life of Donne, a worthy churchman, to provide a preface to his sermons.

Perhaps a more significant example of the early biography of literary men is Johnson's *Lives of the English Poets.* Abrams notes that a *Life* by Johnson usually falls into three parts: first a record of the biographical facts, second an "appraisal of the poet's intellectual character," and last a critical examination of the poems.[9] Johnson seldom allows these three aspects of his writing to invade each other as, say, a nineteenth-century biographer of Byron or Shelley would. Among these later biographers it is often difficult to tell which is their aim—to allow the life to explain the poetry or the poetry to explain the life. In the last analysis, of course, an expressive theory of poetry carried to its extreme blurs the difference.

5. *A less extreme form of expressive theory insists that bio-*

[9] Abrams, *op. cit.,* p. 232.

*graphical information helps us to understand a poem because it can uncover the author's intention in writing it.* One critical issue that arises here is whether or not achievement of an intention insures the success of a poem. A related problem is whether or not failure to achieve what was intended necessarily makes the poem a failure. These questions and others led W. K. Wimsatt and M. C. Beardsley to write their essay, "The Intentional Fallacy," in which they state several propositions: First, a poem is not an accidental creation.[10] An intellect designs it, but this does not logically imply that the standard of judgment should be how well the poem approximates its original design (if, indeed, poems have original designs). Second, there is, as we have seen, the empirical dilemma of discovering what the intention was in the first place. Third, a poem does not appear to be like a message, which *is* judicable by how well it accomplishes its intention. (We are reminded here of Paul Valéry's distinction between walking and dancing.) Fourth, although the meaning of a poem is, of course, a personal one, nevertheless we should not forget that a poem is a dramatic structure and that the speaker may not be the poet. He may best be thought of as a character in a drama. Fifth, when an author revises he may better achieve his intention, but the intention of the revision is "to write a better work." The intention in any other sense changes with revision. This adds another variable to the situation.

Wimsatt and Beardsley see the "intentional fallacy" growing out of the Romantic movement. They draw a distinction between "external and internal evidence for the meaning of a poem"; internal evidence is public (that is, available) and discoverable in the semantics and syntax of the poem, through our knowledge of the language, while external evidence is "private and idiosyncratic; not a part of the work as a linguistic fact." This latter sort includes revelations about why the poet wrote the poem, obtainable from letters, journals, reported conversations, and so forth. There is a third type, similar to external evidence, that is evidence about "the character of the author or about private or semi-private meanings attached to words or topics by an author or by a coterie of which he is a member." Wimsatt and Beardsley hold that a critic primarily interested in internal evidence and moderately interested in type three will produce a criticism far different from that of a critic interested in external evidence and in type three as it shades into external evidence.

[10] In W. K. Wimsatt, *The Verbal Icon* (Lexington: Univ. of Kentucky Press, 1954), pp. 3–18.

They present John Livingston Lowes' study of Coleridge, *The Road to Xanadu,* as an example of the latter.

From the point of view of rigidly "objective" critics like Wimsatt and Beardsley, Lowes's book is indeed a disappointment, for it constantly threatens to reduce the poem it is discussing to a congeries of sources in Coleridge's reading without much respect for the curious way in which the material (if that is what it may be called) is transformed (if that is really what happens) into the poem he wrote. All of the information uncovered about Coleridge's sources does not, of course, change a word in his poem. But this fact does not necessarily negate the usefulness of such information for it may help us in some way or other to discover meanings in the words that we might not have apprehended, meanings special to a time and place. It is clear that to understand a poem we want to understand all the implications of its language. Even laundry lists may be helpful in this matter. The poem is intricately related to the verbal culture from which it springs and which it helps to create.

The external evidence described by Wimsatt and Beardsley may or may not be helpful to understanding a poem, depending upon the poem and how the evidence is used. When the evidence somehow replaces the poem in the critic's eyes there is abundant cause to ask why the critic is bothering with the poem at all. He might have to admit that the poem is for him only evidence to help explore the life and mind of the poet, who is the real object of his concern.

Perhaps the ultimate expressive theory is that of the Italian philosopher Benedetto Croce (1866–1952). I shall concern myself here with the early Croce of the *Aesthetic* (1901). Croce insists on the identity of intuition and expression. He defines intuition first by distinguishing it from intellectual assertion. One manages this distinction by considering the totality of effect aimed at by the author. For example, the anecdotes and effusions in Schopenhauer do not deter us from calling his works intellectual statements. By the same token, intuitive works may contain concepts yet remain intuitive. At first, Croce seems vague about how we are to determine the author's aim or intention. But soon we recognize that he means for us not to ask the author but to look at his work. He believes, in fact, that the intention of the author is inevitably achieved, because all expression *is* intuition. One does not really have an intuition until one has expressed it. This being the case, the intention is inevitably embodied in the expression. There is no question of discovering the intention elsewhere than in the work. In fact, the intention is not *in* the work, it *is* the work.

By intuition Croce means the "undifferentiated unity of the perception of the real and the simple image of the possible." [11] In this definition we see him arriving at something similar to Coleridge's unifying secondary imagination, contrasted to the intellect or analytic power: "In our intuitions we do not oppose ourselves as empirical beings to external reality, but we simply objectify our impressions, whatever they may be." When intuitions are not expressed, they are not intuitions at all but "sensation and mere natural fact." For this reason there are no mute inglorious Miltons. A similar attitude is frequently expressed among modern critics and poets. W. H. Auden has written:

> *How can I know what I think till I see what I say?* A poet writes "The chestnut's comfortable root," and then changes this to "The chestnut's customary root." In this alteration there is no question of replacing one emotion by another, or of strengthening an emotion, but of discovering what the emotion is. The emotion is unchanged, but waiting to be identified like a telephone number one cannot remember.[12]

Croce seems friendly to philosophers who find language to be constitutive of our reality: Thinking depends on the ability to employ language, to symbolize. Man is separated from the other animals by this ability. He is, as Ernst Cassirer has remarked, a symbolizing animal before he is a rational animal. Croce has apparently managed to escape the problem of intention raised by Wimsatt and Beardsley, judging from the position expressed in the first chapters of the *Aesthetic*. Later on we discover remarks that make us pause.

After insisting on the identity of intuition and expression, Croce seems to play fast and loose with the sense he has given to expression. Suddenly he adds a component to artistic creation that he has previously included in expression. This is "externalization." He had made the actual painting of a Madonna or the writing of a poem the expression. Now he insists that some intuition-expressions are externalized and some apparently are not. Externalization he describes as a volitional act: "We cannot will or not will our aesthetic vision: we can however will or not will to externalize it, or rather, to preserve

[11] Quotations from Croce are from *Aesthetic,* tr. by Douglas Áinslee (New York: Noonday Press, 1963).

[12] W. H. Auden, "Squares and Oblongs" in Charles D. Abbot, ed., *Poets at Work* (New York: Harcourt, Brace & World, 1948), pp. 171–81.

and communicate to others, or not, the externalization produced." So mute inglorious Miltons are possible, after all! They
have intuitions, they express them, they may or may not externalize them. It is difficult to see what expression means if it does
not imply externalization, if only to the butcher, the doctor,
the neighbor.

What Croce is trying to do here is allow for the element
of specific artistic technique. Externalization surely involves
technique. But for Croce technique is really *"that romance itself,* or *that new picture* itself and nothing else." It is difficult
to determine whether Croce's apparent shift from a unified
sense of intention, intuition, and expression (in which is included
externalization) on the one hand and intuition-expression separate from externalization on the other is a paradox, an illogical-
ity, or an example of pluralistic points of view in which one
formulation may be true from one vantage and another formulation from another.

If we are to take the last view, perhaps it is possible to say
that in Croce there is both an inner and outer expression,
the latter designated externalization. These two forms of expression would correspond roughly to Coleridge's primary and
secondary imagination—the first always present in all men, the
second at work in the artist when he attempts to construct his
expression in the medium. We tend to accept internal expression
on faith and personal experience but it is of no use to the critic,
because we can never study it, measure it, or criticize it. Therefore, from the critic's vantage the only expression is the work
itself, the externalized expression, which the critic must take as
identical with internal expression—if he is to cling to the idea
of expression at all.

I am not sure that this approach gets Croce out of trouble. It
may only express the difficulty in a new way. When Croce
speaks of "the collection of technical knowledge at the service of
artists desirous of externalizing their expressions," he seems to
have returned us to the same problems we have already en-
countered in expressive theories. The intention, if it is separated
from the externalization, could be changed radically or corrupted
by technique; as a result the work might no longer be the intuition and the poet's intention could no longer be considered
carried out. Croce does not return us to the concept of content
as essentially discursive, such as we find in didactic theories, but
his view does come dangerously close to suggesting that the
same intuition might be conveyed by two different technical

means. Has he closed the breach between form and content? Or has he moved dangerously at the last moment toward an attitude that in the past saw technique as essentially decorative of a separable content? Perhaps any criticism starting from an examination of the poet must eventually pay a price.

In spite of these difficulties Croce's own criticism of hedonistic, moralistic, and intellectualistic aesthetics is powerful. He effectively dismisses theories that emphasize pleasure, moral correctness, or verifiable conceptual statement as bases for aesthetic judgment. He is extremely important as a link between the expressive tradition of the Romantics and the objectivist criticism of the twentieth century. His initial dismissal of the difference between intuition and expression leads us finally away from the poet into the work itself, which becomes the only place the poet's intention can be found. Although he speaks constantly of the activity of the artist, he sees this activity only in what the artist has done.

I wish to emphasize this point because the view of the expressive orientation offered here has perhaps been too negative and concerned solely with its theoretical imperfections. Taken not as a final position but instead as part of a historical development that revealed new possibilities as well as new problems, it is a very important one. First, it effected an escape from a naive emphasis upon the affective aspects of literature, particularly the didactic. If at times it overemphasized undifferentiated feelings as the essence of the poem, at least it made room for the feelings. Second, for this very reason, it sharpened the distinction between literature and other forms of linguistic expression. It did this in an excessively rigid way, perhaps, but at least it did it in a way that sought to give literature a specific nature and unique function. Third, it threw emphasis upon the mental processes involved in poetic activity with interesting implications for later views of what literature is and does and what human nature is.

No one now doubts that the poem is intimately related to its author in many ways worthy of study. The question with which we have been concerned, however, is not that but whether for critical interpretation and judgment this relationship must not be looked on with a certain skepticism, whether for practical purposes and on sound theoretical ground the critic should not be willing at crucial moments, like the God of Anatole France's *Penguin Island,* to forget consciously what he knows in some way inevitably to be true.

# 5 MEANING AND BEING

It is now possible to summarize a major problem that has emerged from our consideration so far. It is the problem of separable content or the split between content and form. Didactic theories and theories of naive imitation suggest a separate conceptual content in the poem. This leads to the conclusion that the poem is decorated by its form and the techniques employed in its writing. The implication is that the poem exists to convey a concept that could be expressed with no essential loss if the decorations were different or even absent or if the concept itself were present in different words. Even theories emphasizing intuition or emotion rather than information suggest a separate emotive or intuitional "thing" to be conveyed. It is implied that in the transfer of this emotion to language, technique is again a means to the conveyance of the emotion with the result that again content and form are separated. The difficulty with the separation, and the reason modern critics have sought to obliterate the idea of it, is that in the first instance poetry would seem to be reduced to philosophy, history, or science merely decorated by frills of language. In the second, poetry would seem to require none of the conventions of logic and would be reduced to mere interjection.

The difficulty can be formulated in another way as the problem of distinguishing poetry from other things, mainly positivistic science, which in the nineteenth century had threatened to take over the whole ground of human knowledge. Imitative and didactic theories seemed to fall into the trap of making poetry essentially decorated conceptual statement. A conceptual statement is verifiable scientifically or subject to analysis of its logical form. If poetry is conceptual, it falls under the tyranny of rational proof. In reaction against this conceptualism Romantic criticism moved toward distinguishing between science as statement of fact and poetry as expression of feeling. There was something desperate in this distinction. With rationality captured by science it seemed that only the area of feeling remained to the poet, and theorists retreated to it. One trouble with the distinction, put this way and only this way, was that according to the popular epistemology (still essentially Lockean) the feelings were subjective and unreal, and poetry, cut off from intellect, seemed diminished in importance. Another trouble was that the distinction appeared to sanction formlessness and sentimentality in poetry. The Romantic poet has often been accused of vagueness leading into realms of generality and abstraction. The only way out of this seemed for a time to be the unacceptable one of returning poetry to the domination of concepts, which are built up by generalization and abstraction. Theory and practice would come full circle, and the tyranny of the rational proof of poetry's propositions would again prevail.

Criticism was still suffering from the distinction well illustrated by Samuel Johnson's insistence that the poet does not, like the scientist, look at the particular, but instead proceeds to the universal. He does not "number the streaks of the tulip"; instead he makes an abstract from his sense experience.

Now Johnson was half right: The poet does not *number* the streaks of the tulip. William Wordsworth was surely correct to rewrite the last few of these lines from "The Thorn":

> High on a mountain's highest ridge,
> Where oft the stormy winter gale
> Cuts like a scythe, while through the clouds
> It sweeps from vale to vale;
> Not five yards from the mountain path,
> This thorn you on your left espy;
> And to your left, three yards beyond,
> You see a little muddy pond,
> Though but of compass small, and bare
> To thirsty suns and parching air.
> I've measured it from side to side;
> 'Tis three feet long, and two feet wide.

But Johnson was quite wrong in thinking he had made a real distinction, for the numbering and measuring functions are classifiable *with* and not *in contrast to* the abstracting and generalizing functions.

Later critics would make their distinction between science and poetry in a different way. They would not distinguish precise, particular scientific fact from vague, unspecified poetic feeling. Instead they would distinguish science, which proceeds toward the abstract and general, from poetry, which inhabits the concrete and particular. The process of reorganizing these terms into the appropriate columns, so to speak, took more than a century, perhaps because the original distinction seemed to have common sense on its side.

In his book *The New Apologists for Poetry,* Murray Krieger has characterized the earlier criticism with words and phrases that I shall place in two opposing columns:

| SCIENCE | POETRY |
|---|---|
| denotative adequacy | unbridled connotation |
| logicality | lack of argumentative progression |
| precision | vagueness |
| intellect | imagination or intuition |
| reason | emotion |
| truth to particular reality | truth to the ideal and universal [1] |

These distinctions are observed by the German Romantic theorists who strove to equate the beautiful in art with expression of the infinite. Even as Romantic critics accepted these distinctions, however, they struggled boldly with them, attempting to make the infinite *inhabit* the particular rather than to allow the poem to wander off into the abstract ether of generalization.

Friedrich von Schelling perhaps exemplifies the struggle in its early Romantic stages as well as anyone. He is skeptical of servile imitation because he sees no truly creative act in it:

> in all things in Nature, the living idea shows itself only blindly active; were it so also in the artist, he would be in nothing distinct from Nature. But, should he attempt consciously to subordinate himself altogether to the Actual, and render with servile fidelity the already existing, he would produce *larvae,* but no works of Art.[2]

For Schelling, the alternative is to escape the actual only to re-

[1] Murray Krieger, *The New Apologists for Poetry* (Minneapolis: Univ. of Minnesota Press, 1956), p. 140.

[2] Quotations from Schelling are from "On the Relation of the Plastic Arts to Nature," tr. by J. Elliott Cabot.

turn to Nature, having transformed it by infusing it with the ideal:

> He must therefore withdraw himself from the product, from the creation, but only in order to raise himself to the creative energy, spiritually seizing the same. Thus he ascends into the realm of pure ideas; he forsakes the creation, to regain it with thousandfold interest, and in this sense certainly to return to Nature. This spirit of Nature working at the core of things, and speaking through form and shape as by symbols only, the artist must certainly follow with emulation; and only so far as he seizes this with genial imitation has he himself produced anything genuine. For works produced by aggregation, even of forms beautiful in themselves, would still be destitute of all beauty, since that through which the work on the whole is truly beautiful cannot be mere form—it is Essence, the Universal, the look and expression of the indwelling spirit of Nature.

Schelling holds that art seeks the transcendent and universal, while at the same time he wants to find the universal dwelling in, immanent in, particulars. He cannot quite get these two ideas joined; the universal tends to dominate, as it does generally among Romantic theorists. The common, prosaic, particular world is thought to be transcended by spiritual art that employs the images of this world, finally, to attain to infinite experience. The idea of immanence is constantly devoured by the idea that things are merely symbols for infinite truths, which returns us again to the abstract.

Thomas Carlyle (1795–1881) exemplifies the attitude in *Sartor Resartus:* "In the Symbol proper, what we can call a Symbol, there is ever, more or less distinctly and directly, some embodiment and revelation of the Infinite; the Infinite is made to blend itself with the Finite, to stand visible, and as it were, attainable there." His idea of a symbol is closer to the definition of allegory made by Johann Wolfgang von Goethe in his well-known remark distinguishing allegory and symbolism:

> It makes a great difference whether the poet starts with a universal idea and then looks for suitable particulars, or beholds the universal *in* the particular. The former method produces allegory, where the particular has status merely as an instance, an example of the universal. The latter, by contrast, is what reveals poetry in its true nature: it speaks forth a particular without independently thinking of or referring to a universal, but in grasping the particular in its living character it implicitly apprehends the universal along with it.[3]

[3] From *Conversations with Eckermann,* entry dated October 29, 1823.

Goethe here is thinking like Blake, who attacked allegory as an example of Locke's false epistemology and insisted that all knowledge was of particulars. This did not, of course, prevent Blake from equivocating and calling one of his prophetic books a "sublime allegory" or from writing poems that invited interpretation on a variety of levels. But he stoutly held that his universal truths were always particular, joining these two terms in a paradox that writers from Georg Hegel to W. K. Wimsatt have sought by a variety of stratagems to hold together.[4]

If we return to Carlyle for a moment we recall that for him the symbol seems a sort of shorthand for an abstraction, like a Platonic idea. Poetry that moves to express abstractions is reducible again to the old form-content division, with the content a concept. This is one of the reasons, perhaps, that Goethe refused the label of "romantic"; "I call the classic *healthy,* the romantic *sickly,*" he said.[5] Twentieth-century criticism, which to some extent was ushered in by T. E. Hulme (1883–1917), began as anti-Romantic in a similar vein. In his *Speculations,* Hulme, fiercely critical of the Romantic poets, whom he characterized as always flying away into the "circumambient gas," remarked:

> The essence of poetry to most people is that it must lead them to a beyond of some kind. Verse strictly confined to the earthly and the definite (Keats is full of it) might seem to them to be excellent writing, excellent craftsmanship, but not poetry. So much has romanticism debauched us, that, without some sort of vagueness, we deny the highest.[6]

Hulme also objects to "the sloppiness which doesn't consider that a poem is a poem unless it is moaning or whining about something or other." [7] In short, he rejects the idea of the poem's concrete language as merely standing for or leading to the infinite, a poem that, seeking the infinite, soars into generalization and abstraction, and a poem that is emotion at the total expense of reason. We can see at once that the two columns or sets of phrases and words supplied to describe an earlier criticism's distinction between science and poetry must be drastically revised to accommodate Hulme.

---

[4] See especially W. K. Wimsatt, "The Concrete Universal" in *The Verbal Icon* (Lexington: Univ. of Kentucky Press, 1954), pp. 69–83.

[5] *Conversations with Eckermann,* entry dated April 2, 1829.

[6] T. E. Hulme, "Romanticism and Classicism" in *Speculations* (New York: Harcourt, Brace & World, n.d., first published 1924), p. 127.

[7] *Ibid.,* p. 120.

Indeed, the columns were gradually revised by twentieth-century critics, who chose to maintain the old Romantic distinction between science and poetry but to talk of it as a distinction between uses of language, not between disembodied modes of thought:

| SCIENTIFIC LANGUAGE | POETIC LANGUAGE |
| --- | --- |
| denotative adequacy | contextual organization |
| logical precision | metaphorical fitness |
| generalization | concretion |
| truth to the ideal and universal | truth to particular reality |

The last pair, we notice, has interchanged sides.

Early twentieth-century criticism also separated the poem from the poet, seeking to make irrelevant the vague, indefinable realm of the poet's emotions. It moved toward treating the poem as an object, composed of language, discussible intelligently *as* an order of language. In effecting these shifts it was trying to evade certain traditional positions. These we have examined, but it is helpful to summarize them here in the way that Krieger does:[8]

1. Poetry is not propositional and is therefore worthless. (The purely Platonic position.)
2. Poetry is propositional and is thus allegorical or decorated conceptual statement. (The position implicit in Philip Sidney's remarks about allegory and in later theories that imply a separable rational content.)
3. Poetry simply gives pleasure. (The other side of the Platonic coin, in which propositional truth is either willingly or under duress of science discarded in favor of the idea of poetry as instrumental, not of knowledge, but of pleasure—that is, of transport, as in Longinus, of delight, and of therapy. The position is usually referred to as aesthetic hedonism.

The problem was to restate a fourth position apparent in Romantic theory. Poetry gives not propositional truth but imaginative truth. But just what is "imaginative truth"? The term had to be kept from being interpreted to mean Platonic abstraction, for that would return criticism to the second or third position stated above or to the idea of poetry as expression of sheer emotion.

The twentieth-century critics with whom we are shortly to be

[8] Krieger, *op. cit.*, pp. 170–72.

concerned tried to think of the poem as an autonomous object. The poem has, in the words of John Crowe Ransom, an ontological status, a special mode of being. These critics realized, of course, that every poem has an author and a reader, but they recognized the formidable difficulties that have always dogged theories emphasizing the poem's relationship to either. They wished to preserve the importance of the poem in relation to the world around it, but they did not want to confuse the poem with science. They sought to look into the poem as a linguistic object with its own laws; they refused to admit the author's intention to their consideration; they would not distinguish between his intuition and his externalization; if intuition and expression had any meaning for them it was only *as* the externalization itself, complete with technique. They held that the poem is a construction of language different from other kinds of linguistic constructions; they asserted that poetry is not concerned with the world of scientific generalization, the world of Platonic forms, Kantian noumena or things in themselves, or whatever is beyond the particular.

How critics came to this position has been touched upon in the brief discussions of imitation and creation, universals and particulars, allegory and symbolism. Here it is important to backtrack and look briefly at some nineteenth-century developments proceeding from Immanuel Kant. Kant's two important contributions to modern critical theory are as follows: First, in the realm of epistemology he proposed that the mind is to some extent constitutive of the phenomenal world. It operates through the *a priori* forms and the categories of the understanding (*verstand*) upon the manifold of sensation. We cannot know things in themselves, but it is possible for science to exist under the terms by which the understanding organizes experience. This idea of the constitutive power of the mind put forward in the *Critique of Pure Reason* influenced Schelling, Coleridge, the other Romantic writers, and the Symbolists; almost all literary theory since has had to take account of it.

Second, in the realm of aesthetics, Kant established the idea of the universality of an aesthetic judgment that "does not rest on concepts of objects." Aesthetic judgment is not cognitive. If I conclude that a particular rose is beautiful, that is an aesthetic judgment. If I conclude that roses are beautiful, that involves a concept and is a logical judgment based on an aesthetic or several aesthetic judgments. In the *Critique of Judgment* Kant points out that all aesthetic judgments are singular and argues:

> There can be no objective rule of taste which shall determine by
> means of concepts what is beautiful. For every judgment from
> this source is aesthetical; i.e., the feeling of the subject, and not a
> concept of the object, is its determining ground. To seek for a
> principle of taste which shall furnish, by means of definite con-
> cepts, a universal criterion of the beautiful is fruitless trouble,
> because what is sought is impossible and self-contradictory.[9]

This view supports metaphors of organism that developed among
Romantic critics to describe poems. Poems are seen, according to
this metaphor, as objects that generate their own principles of
order. Kant releases the work of art from purposiveness; that is,
he does not consider that it exists to convey concepts. If in any
sense it can be thought to present ideas, these ideas are "aesthetical ideas" that call for the reader to contemplate them but do
not produce concepts adequate to express their meaning. It seems
to follow that the aesthetical idea is only the poem itself. Kant
doesn't quite say this, but he does say: "By an aesthetical idea I
understand that representation of the imagination which occa-
sions much thought, without however any definite thought, i.e.
any *concept*, being capable of being adequate to it; it consequently cannot be completely compassed and made intelligible
by language." [10] By "language" here it is possible to read Kant
to mean language used cognitively or logically, and to infer that
the poet has employed language in a different way. This suggests
that we cannot bring the poem to judgment by applying any
exterior conceptual standards to it.

Kant goes on to talk about the poet's activity in a way vaguely
reminiscent of Sidney but from a totally different vantage point.
The poet creates "another nature, as it were, out of the material
that actual nature gives it." The poet makes "something different
which surpasses nature":

> Such representations of the imagination we may call *ideas*, partly
> because they at least strive after something which lies beyond the
> bounds of experience and so seek to approximate to a presenta-
> tion of concepts of reason (intellectual ideas), thus giving to the
> latter the appearance of objective reality, but especially because
> no concept can be fully adequate to them as internal intuitions.
> The poet ventures to realize, to sense rational ideas of invisible
> beings, the kingdom of the blessed, hell, eternity, creation, etc;
> or even if he deals with things of which there are examples in

[9] Immanuel Kant, *Critique of Judgment*, tr. by J. H. Bernard (New York:
Hafner, 1951), p. 68.
[10] *Ibid.*, p. 157.

experience—e.g. death, envy and all vices, also love, fame, and the like—he tries, by means of imagination, which emulates the play of reason in its quest after a maximum, to go beyond the limits of experience and to present them to sense with a completeness of which there is no example in nature.[11]

Without proceeding to a long commentary on the *Critique of Judgment,* including a discussion of what Kant means by reason, let me suggest that both Kant's epistemology and aesthetic influenced Coleridge, but the epistemology had a strong infusion of Schelling's *System of Transcendental Idealism.* Greatly influenced by Kant, Schelling nevertheless refused to accept Kant's idea of the total unavailability to the mind of things in themselves. Schelling proposed a realm of spirit, the highest reality, in which the mind as subject marries itself to things in themselves as objects. This marriage *is* artistic intuition; art is the product of the marriage.

If we say that Coleridge's epistemology in *Biographia Literaria,* where long passages are translations of Schelling, is after Schelling, we must add that his discussion of the beautiful in the *Principles of Genial Criticism* is very Kantian indeed. Coleridge's source is the *Critique of Judgment,* and he establishes the freedom of the work of art from concepts of the understanding and from purposiveness.

On the one hand, then, we have a Schellingean Coleridge who sees the poem as a linguistic representation of the highest spiritual act, the poet's marriage of mind and object. (The poem is not the act itself, apparently.) On the other hand, we have a Coleridge who sees the poem in a Kantian way as having no exterior object or act to which it refers, only an interior aesthetical idea that it creates by its own nature and which is untranslatable from it.

Most Romantic criticism and practice is closer to the Schellingean Coleridge than the Kantian, although one senses several theorists trying to escape Schelling's idea of the poem's subservience to the spiritual reality it is supposed to stand for. Carlyle discussing symbolism is an example, but he ends up indicating, as we have seen, that the poetic symbol bodies forth the infinite. From these critics there follows all that Hulme objected to—namely that Romantic poets were "unable to admit the existence of beauty without the infinite being in some way or another dragged in":

[11] *Ibid.,* pp. 157–58.

Particularly in Germany, the land where theories of aesthetics were first created, the romantic aesthetes collated all beauty to an impression of the infinite involved in the identification of our being in absolute spirit. In the least element of beauty we have a total intuition of the whole world. Every artist is a kind of pantheist.[12]

Hulme would detach beauty from Schelling's metaphysical absolute and discover it in the finite, not as a symbol there of the infinite but simply as itself. Hulme talks about the artist's struggle with language, and he almost, but not quite, says that the artist experiences by means of language rather than by having an experience and then expressing it in the poem. Through the nineteenth century the Symbolists in France were struggling with the same idea.

It has already been noted that Charles Baudelaire asked questions in his art criticism that were fundamental to the doctrine of imitation and the location of reality. He announced it possible to prefer the "monsters of [his] fancy to what is positively trivial," and he went on to question the existence of nature except in so far as the imagination constructs it.[13] But there is a sort of mystical element in Baudelaire that leads him to suggest that the imagination uses poetry as a vehicle to express through the visibilia of the universe, not the infinite of the German Romantics, but some occult spiritual reality not otherwise apprehensible: "The whole visible universe is but a storehouse of images and signs to which the imagination will give a relative place and value; it is a sort of pasture which the imagination must digest and transform." [14] As a result Baudelaire seems to let himself in for the same criticism that Hulme makes of the Romantics. In theory the poem seems dependent on how well it represents to us this occult world, which is, for Baudelaire, more real than the world of cold, inanimate nature bequeathed by materialistic science to nineteenth-century man. The idea is clearly expressed in his famous sonnet "Correspondences."

A similar sense of the poem as a representation of an occult superreality occurs in Stephane Mallarmé (1842–98), but it is curiously hedged around and qualified. We sense his desire to say that the poem does not introduce us to something occult existing beyond it but that it generates its own mystery, its own reality,

---

[12] Hulme, *op. cit.*, p. 131.
[13] Charles Baudelaire, "The Queen of the Faculties" in *The Mirror of Art*, tr. and ed. by Jonathan Mayne (New York: Doubleday, 1956), p. 233.
[14] Baudelaire, "The Governance of the Imagination," *ibid.*, p. 241.

that is more real than anything it seems to be copying. In "Mystery in Literature," he begins ironically:

> Every work of art, apart from its inner treasure, should provide some sort of outward—or even indifferent—meaning through its words. A certain deference should be shown the people; for, after all, they are lending out their language . . . . And yet somehow there is a disquieting gleam from the depths of the work, hardly distinguishable from its outward show. The clever idlers become suspicious and tell us to stop; for in their considered opinion the meaning of the work is unintelligible.[15]

And he proceeds ironically, making his way precariously between the idea that a poem is completely autonomous and creates its own indwelling mystery and the idea that the poem builds up a representation (however lurking or insubstantial) of a spiritual reality external to it. He occasionally comes down strongly on the side of the poem's making reality: He proposes that the obscurity that is his poem "may be a reality; that it may exist, for example, on a piece of paper, in a piece of writing." [16] He argues:

> Up to now, writers have entertained the childish belief that if they could just choose a certain number of precious stones, for example, and set the names on paper, they would be making precious stones. Now, really! that is impossible, no matter how well it is done. Poetry is *creation*.[17]

But he doesn't stay put. The poem in his mind tends to represent a state of soul: "And if, in fact, the precious stones we wear do *not* show a state of soul, they are improperly worn." [18] The poem is not after all quite freed from the external object it expresses.

Nevertheless, most of the time Mallarmé sees the poem as autonomous and the poetic symbol as that element in the poem the meaning of which is made by its context, untranslatable out of that context.

But once he makes the poem autonomous, Mallarmé does not establish clearly enough for us what its value is. When he tries to do so, he returns to his idea of the poem as a representation of a mysterious state of soul that is accessible only through the poem. Later critics will try to get around this problem. Paul Valéry's dis-

---

[15] Stephane Mallarmé, *Selected Prose Poems, Essays, and Letters,* tr. by Bradford Cook (Baltimore: Johns Hopkins, 1956), p. 29.
[16] *Ibid.,* p. 30.
[17] Mallarmé, "The Evolution of Literature," *ibid.,* p. 23.
[18] *Ibid.*

tinction between walking and dancing is an attempt to preserve the autonomy of the work of art as well as to establish its own unique value by describing it as a *mode of language* different from that of scientific and logical modes. We now turn to those twentieth-century critics who exploit this distinction and try to maintain the poem's autonomy while still insisting that the poem gives us knowledge.

In Chaper 1, we observed that criticism has often advanced by negation, by the sloughing away of inadequate ideas. Such advances have usually been achieved, however, by combating earlier attitudes while actually appropriating aspects of these attitudes. Those critics associated with the New Criticism of the thirties and forties were anti-Romantic, following Hulme and with help from T. S. Eliot. They rejected Schelling's universal and the realm of infinite spirit; they hated Romantic vagueness and sentimentality; yet they maintained, with some very important variations, the Romantic distinction between science and poetry.

They were also in the debt of Benedetto Croce. The Crocean aesthetic, with its emphasis on the poet-poem relationship (a relationship ignored as much as possible by the New Critics) brought the author's intuition and expression together only to break it apart again by adding the element of externalization. This valiant struggle to give art a specific function did emphasize the difference between art and science. Although the Crocean aesthetic failed ultimately to obliterate the distinction between form and content, it took at least a step toward the idea of the poem as an untranslatable unity. In its failure it carried the expressive theory to the limit and by negation influenced critics who would approach the poem through the externalization, through the language, rather than through the inevitably vague and unlocatable intuition of the author.

Another critic whose influence on the New Criticism cannot be overestimated is I. A. Richards. Yet Richards' psychologism and naive materialism came under attack from the same critics he influenced. His early theorizing in the *Principles of Literary Criticism* tried to locate the poem in the reader's response or in the artist's ability to organize his own feelings. Neither location brought into consideration what for the New Critics was the paramount issue: the artist's struggle with the real material of his art, language. Richards held that poetry aims to arouse feelings in the reader and the more feelings it arouses and the greater the equilibrium of these feelings, the better the experience.

Richards' problem was that he tried to talk of the poem as if it were actually locatable in the feelings and attitudes of the poet or in the feelings of the reader. The poem itself seemed to have for him no objective existence.

But without the poem itself what are the feelings? Can they be talked about at all? Here Croce's remarks are helpful, for at one stage of his *Aesthetic* he seemed to be claiming that whatever was to go into the poem was nothing until it was in the poem or was the poem. The problem was to transfer somehow what Richards had to say about the feelings and impulses and emotions into a discussion of the poem as a specific object; for Richards had said some interesting things, particularly about irony. In the *Principles of Literary Criticism* Richards, with his characteristic behaviorist jargon, argues that there are two ways in which impulses may be ordered, by elimination and by synthesis. Much poetry orders limited experiences, excluding others. Such poetry may be admirable, but it is not great. Tennyson's "Break, Break, Break" and Landor's "Rose Aylmer" are examples. The greater, synthetic poem is exemplified by Keats's "Ode to a Nightingale," "Sir Patrick Spens," and Marvell's "The Definition of Love." Richards draws the following distinction:

> The structures of these two kinds of experiences are different, and the difference is not one of subject but of relations *inter se* of the several impulses active in the experience. A poem of the first group is built out of sets of impulses which run parallel, which have the same direction. In a poem of the second group the most obvious feature is the extraordinarily [*sic*] heterogeneity of the distinguishable impulses. But they are more than heterogeneous, they are opposed.[19]

These remarks lead to Richards' definition of irony: "bringing in of the opposite, the complementary impulses." [20] Richards has trouble locating all this in the poem because of his vague psychologistic language, which never touches upon the problems of the medium, of specifically literary construction. A separation between the impulses in the poem and the medium is implied.

For the New Critics who read him, however, Richards reduced his own position to absurdity. They transferred the balance of impulses, which for Richards resided somewhere in the limbo of the author's attitude or reader's response, into the structure of

[19] I. A. Richards, *Principles of Literary Criticism* (New York: Harcourt, Brace & World, 1925).
[20] *Ibid.*

the poem. They did not dwell on the artist's ability to have complexities of feeling. They were interested in the artist only insofar
as he dealt with the materials that made the poem.

Perhaps the leading figure of the New Criticism was John
Crowe Ransom, poet, professor, founder and longtime editor of
the *Kenyon Review*. In three books and numerous essays and
reviews Ransom tried to center critical activity upon the poem
as an objective thing.[21] Consistent with the general anti-Romantic
effort to redeem poetry from pure emotion devoid of reason,
Ransom rejected both the idea that scientific activity was unemo-
tional and the idea that poetic activity was completely irrational.
He objected to those who were willing to surrender "the honor
of objectivity" to science if they might have "the luxury of subjectivity" for poetry. Just as poetry possesses logic and a cognitive
element, so is science an activity based upon feeling, as all activity
is. Else, it would never have been undertaken in the first place.
Ransom suggested that, as critics, we must forget feelings and
attend to the poetic object. He was particularly critical of
Richards' psychologizing, and he saw little practical use in Eliot's
idea of the "objective correlative," something in the work of art
("a set of objects, a situation, a chain of events") that supplies a
sort of formula to convey a particular desired emotion:[22]

> There may be a feeling correlative with the minutest alteration
> in an object, and adequate to it, but we shall hardly know. What
> we do know is that the feelings are grossly inarticulate if we try to
> abstract them and take their testimony in their own language.
> Since it is not the intent of the critic to be inarticulate, his dis-
> criminations must be among the objects.[23]

Eliot's terminology was too vague for Ransom, yet he was sym-
pathetic with Eliot and provided a translation of Eliot's own
psychological language into terms referable only to the poem
itself, not to either the author or the reader. Ransom held that if

[21] The critical books of Ransom are *God Without Thunder* (New York: Harcourt, Brace & World, 1930), *The World's Body* (New York: Scribner's, 1938),
*The New Criticism* (New York: New Directions, 1941), *Poems and Essays*
(New York: Random House, 1955).
[22] T. S. Eliot, "Hamlet and His Problems" in *Selected Essays 1917–1932* (New
York: Harcourt, Brace & World, 1950), pp. 124–25.
[23] John Crowe Ransom, "Criticism as Pure Speculation" in Donald A.
Stauffer, ed., *The Intent of the Critic* (Gloucester, Mass.: Peter Smith, 1963),
p. 97.

Eliot had used more accurate language, he would have said that the poem has a sort of central logic or situation or "paraphrasable core" along with a "context of lively local details to which other and independent interests attach." [24] This formulation announces that the poem is different from scientific discourse because the details of scientific discourse are never properly independent of the thesis or conceptual core. They always function in a way that subordinates them to the conveyance of the thesis.

In his remark about a "paraphrasable core," Ransom seems to have separated form and content all over again. Nevertheless, he succeeded in drawing a distinction of some sort between poetic and scientific uses of language without relegating poetry to pure expression of feeling or locating it in the author's intuition or the reader's response. Ransom's formulation eschews the whining that Hulme found so unpleasant in Romanticism. Ransom's point, though vulnerable to the charge of splitting form and content in theory when in practice the dividing line cannot be found, is an interesting one. In scientific language the ideal is that every detail should contribute to the concept to be formulated; in argument, detail enforces a point by illustration or by emotive appeal. There is in each case a clear purposiveness. In poetry detail may struggle with, even change, the concept, or at least make the concept unimportant as a concept but supremely important as part of the context in which it functions.

Ransom attacked both the moralistic critic, who wants the poem to say something morally acceptable, and the critic who assumes that it makes no difference what the poet says as long as he says it well. The latter position was an unsophisticated version of "art for art's sake," though one not often argued any more. Art for art's sake in its attack on the excesses of moralistic criticism seemed in the popular eye to emasculate art and dissociate it from life. Ransom considered the argument between these two views "an excellent example of how two doctrines, inadequate equally but in opposite senses, may keep themselves alive by abhorring each other's errors." [25] Moralistic criticism fails because, although it is possible to produce a paraphrase of a poem or of a speech from a play or a synopsis of a plot, it is impossible to substitute it for the original. The details irrelevant to logical argument are expandable in ways that do not support the argument, and yet they affect the way the reader wants to

[24] *Ibid.*, p. 98.
[25] *Ibid.*, p. 103.

take it. These details provide what is all-important to the poem, "a sense of the real density and contingency of the world in which arguments and plans have to be pursued." [26]

Ransom challenged an uncompromising, organic theory of poetry that, if rigidly held, would insist that there is nothing we can say about a poem except to repeat it in its own words. Fearing he might fall too far in the other direction, however, he insisted that if the critic has nothing to say about the texture of a poem, he is not really treating it as a poem at all. The poem is an organic whole, but to talk about it we must somehow make the distinction between its logical core and its bundle of textural detail. Then the critical discourse must methodically heal the separation it has made. The way Ransom put this distinction was not quite acceptable to Cleanth Brooks, his student, who saw dangers of "the heresy of paraphrase" in it; but it is the sort of distinction that makes one understand why R. P. Blackmur insisted that a critic should approach the poem by way of its technique.

In an essay in *The World's Body*, Ransom reveals how these critical principles support his taste for metaphysical verse. He speaks of three sorts of poetry: the physical, the Platonic, and the metaphysical.[27] He sees physical poetry, exemplified in recent times by the Imagist school, as an outgrowth of dissatisfaction with the Victorian poetry of ideas. It is a poetry of things, a rejection of abstract concepts as the content to be communicated by poems. The Victorian poetry of ideas is a version of Platonic poetry, which formulates abstract concepts. In such poetry images are illustrations; there is often a tendency toward allegory. A third sort of poetry, the metaphysical, has a tough structure of argument that the poetry of Imagism tends to lack. The metaphysical admits meter, fiction, trope, and metaphor. Its technical elements, the details apparently irrelevant to the poem's logic, turn out to be supremely relevant to the total poem, drawing the reader from paraphrase of the so-called argument back into the poem's density and complexity.

Cleanth Brooks, an apologist for metaphysical and modern poetry in his *Modern Poetry and the Tradition* (1939), developed an organicism even more insistent apparently than Ransom's. For him, the beauty of a poem is "the flowering of the whole

[26] *Ibid.*, p. 107.
[27] See "Poetry: A Note on Ontology" in *The World's Body* (New York: Scribner's, 1938), pp. 111–42.

plant, and needs the stalk, the leaf, and the hidden roots." [28]
Brooks is clearly fascinated by the famous lines about the chestnut
tree, the dancer, and the dance that come at the end of Yeats's
"Among School Children." They are for him, as for others, a sort
of allegory of the poem as organism. In Brooks's criticism the
poem is always to be considered a sort of drama. This is particularly important to remember when it least appears to be
true, specifically in the lyric. There, the reader, steeped in the
Romantic expressive attitude, may be inclined to treat the poem
as an overflowing of the poet's own soul, but this is a mistake.
Each lyric has a speaker who for the sake of the poem must be
separated from the author even when the speaker's name is the
same as that of the author. This is because Brooks sees the context of the poem controlling everything. No statement in a poem
is abstract. Even "two times two equals four" put into a poem
is *said* by someone, and its significance is created by the dramatic
context. Many statements in poems are clearly abstract and conceptual when viewed in isolation, but because they occur in the
context of poems they are not subject to treatment as propositions.
The poet's business is to make this point quite clear. He should
not lead the reader to assume that he should judge the poem
according to whether its detachable statements are true or false,
moral or immoral, and so forth. Brooks's objection to Romantic
poetry and to Shelley in particular is that in Shelley's poetry
"certain statements, explicit or implied, because they are not
properly assimilated to a total context, wrench themselves free
from the context, and demand to be judged on ethical or religious grounds." [29] Brooks adds that the fault, of course, may not
lie with the poet. It may be with the reader who ignores the
context. Much of Richards' *Practical Criticism* is concerned,
with the problem of readers who make stock responses to elements of poems, ignoring how these elements are affected by the
context. Brooks would undoubtedly approve of Coleridge's reply,
recorded in his *Table-Talk,* to Mrs. Barbauld, who had told
him his *Ancient Mariner* was a fine poem but suffered from the
lack of a moral. Coleridge answered that in his opinion the
poem's moral was too obtrusive: "the only or chief fault, if I

[28] Cleanth Brooks, "Irony as a Principle of Structure" in M. D. Zabel, ed.,
*Literary Opinion in America,* Vol. II (New York: Harper and Row, 1962),
p. 729.
[29] Cleanth Brooks, *The Well Wrought Urn* (New York: Harcourt, Brace &
World, 1947), p. 227.

might say so, was the obtrusion of the moral sentiment so openly on the reader as a principle or cause of action in a work of such pure imagination."

The means Brooks offers the poet to escape the failures of Shelley is irony. He does not locate irony where Richards did, in the vague area of the reader's impulses. Irony is a characteristic of the poem itself. Irony for Brooks has a very broad meaning. It is acknowledgment at all times by the poem of the pressure of the context upon any given part of the poem. The poet does not simply choose a theme and embellish it. The true meaning of a poem issues forth from all its particulars in their special configuration. To be *absolutely* truthful, of course, the meaning does not issue forth at all. It *inhabits* the poem. In fact, "being" is probably a better word for what Brooks means than "meaning." From the point of view of conceptual thought, poetic meaning is elusive and the poem proceeds by indirection and metaphor.

In Brooks, then, irony is a word to embody the principal quality of language that separates poetic and conceptual discourse. Poetic language thrives on ambiguity created by the context. It is complex and opaque. Conceptual discourse strives for the unambiguous. Its contextual laws are those of logic. Its language is transparent and referential. Its metaphor is decorative rather than organic.

As a result Brooks attacks "the heresy of paraphrase" as the cause of most critical errors:

> If we allow ourselves to be misled by it, we distort the relation of the poem to its "truth," we raise the problem of belief in a vicious and crippling form, we split the poem between its "form" and its "content"—we bring the statement to be conveyed into an unreal competition with science or philosophy or theology . . . . By taking the paraphrase as our point of stance, we misconceive the function of metaphor and meter. We demand logical coherences where they are sometimes irrelevant, and we fail frequently to see imaginative coherences on levels where they are highly relevant.[30]

Brooks is suspicious of Ransom's "paraphrasable core," worrying that the least inclination to accept paraphrase, whatever the terms, will drag criticism back into the depths of the heresy. At the same time, however, he is willing to say that often we can make paraphrastic formulations in order to get ourselves started talking about the poem. These "scaffoldings" must, however, be

---

[30] Brooks, *The Well Wrought Urn,* pp. 184–85.

torn down so that the true building may properly be seen. On the basis of this qualification, Brooks reveals himself as closer to Ransom than we might have thought. He has acknowledged, as did Ransom, that to talk coherently about a poem is to talk conceptually. The alternative is sage silence or repetition of the poem itself.

Unfortunately, as Ransom pointed out, the paraphrase, the hunting down and the evaluation of the concepts—yanked from their controlling context—is the easier procedure. Few critics can resist its temptations. Brooks's warnings emphasize his desire to keep literature clearly defined and separate from other linguistic forms. The paraphrase can be compared to other forms of discourse and judged by their standards. The poem cannot.

Openness and inclusiveness of mind would seem to be a prerequisite for the critic who seeks to preserve the autonomy of the poem. The critic, as Blackmur's work seems to imply, must not sight literature through a doctrine. In criticism, as in the poem, doctrine is not the completion of insight. This is not to say that Blackmur's criticism has no theoretical base, for every criticism implies some theoretical base, shifting as it may be. It is to say that Blackmur's initial impulse was to bring every sort of knowledge to bear upon the critical act but to allow no body of knowledge to dominate it. The critic must escape from doctrine. He must also be aware of doctrine—the Freudian, the Marxist, and so forth. He may be able to appropriate to his uses the insights upon which these doctrines are based, but he must be able to "discount, absorb, or dominate the doctrine for the life that goes with it." [31] Blackmur abhorred the *idée fixe,* which he defined as "a notion of genuine but small scope . . . taken literally as of universal application." Most escapes from the central critical act use doctrine as a rallying point to examine literature for its "separable content." True criticism is "the formal discourse of an amateur." By "amateur" is meant one who has a vast learning but is not entrapped by doctrines, which feed on learning. The critic cannot be in the pay of an idea. It is clear that Blackmur is with Brooks in his distrust of the paraphrase. At least it should so follow that he is, for his objection to doctrine is similar to the objection to reading poems as conceptual statements. For this reason Blackmur advocated an approach to the poem primarily through its technique. Lest we think this again splits the object into form and content, we

[31] R. P. Blackmur, "A Critic's Job of Work" in *The Lion and the Honeycomb* (New York: Harcourt, Brace & World, 1955), p. 342.

should recognize that in Blackmur's criticism technique *is* the poem. If we approach the poem through it, everything becomes discussible in its terms. The advantage of such an approach is that it clearly helps to avoid treating the poem as merely a conceptual statement. Blackmur argued that other approaches are useful to him when they manage, as they often do, to touch upon technique. This is his advantage: He can gain from the insights of other approaches, but other approaches, whether through content or concept, cannot gain from his, since they already have abstracted out of the poem everything they wish to see.

Because Blackmur had a far-ranging, inquisitive intellect he was particularly aware of the dangers of a good theory in the hands of mechanical practitioners who had not earned it through hard thought and much experience of literature. In the title essay of *The Lion and the Honeycomb* he expressed the fear that the New Criticism with its approach through technique may have spawned a methodology, and only a methodology, for professionals. In his essay Blackmur invented another term for the critic, whom he had previously described as an "amateur" engaged in "formal discourse." The critic was now a "master-layman of as many modes of human understanding as possible in a single act of the mind." [32] The idea of the "professional" practitioner of criticism was anathema to him because it implied unthinking appropriation of a method.

Although Blackmur did not depart significantly from the theoretical base established by Ransom, Brooks, and others, he did complain about what had happened in the application of their principles. The application had grown out of a particular set of interests and a particular culture:

> What is called the "new criticism"—now well enough established to have a public odor of disrepute about it—is, I should expect, a set of emphases in criticism and scholarship which have been objectively determined, like other sets of emphases in other times, by the literature, by the presumed reader, by the general state of culture and knowledge, and by the immediate history and tradition of critical and scholarly ideas and practice: all working unequally and more or less incongruously together. Let us look at some of these determinants, and then at the criticism.[33]

So Blackmur, champion of a technical approach, came finally to an evaluation of the relation between critical methodology and

[32] Blackmur, "The Lion and the Honeycomb," *ibid.,* p. 183.
[33] *Ibid.,* p. 188.

the culture in which it operates. The critic must examine constantly why he is pursuing the method he is pursuing and what his ultimate aims are. In his later work Blackmur commented more frequently on the culture itself. The first essay in *The Lion and the Honeycomb,* called "Toward a Modus Vivendi," concerns itself with the "new illiteracy" that seems to have been spawned by universal education.[34] The result of it has been, according to Blackmur, a growing contempt in which writers, artists, and literacy in general are held. He deplores the "progressive development of physical energy without a corresponding development of intelligence." The "new illiteracy" is created by those taught to read but not to read well or to discover what is worth reading. Criticism's cultural function is to teach us to read well and to determine what is worth reading. Poetry is "not life lived but life formed and identified," making possible judgments upon it and ultimately a *modus vivendi.*

The New Criticism had from the beginning a cultural purpose like that enunciated by Blackmur. Its insistence on poetry as a separate use of language was part of a desire to dissociate it from the dehumanizing positivistic tradition. Among the critics most concerned with this matter was Allen Tate, who in a series of essays insisted that movement into the spiritual realm of materialistic scientific vocabularies, such as that attempted by I. A. Richards in his early criticism, was a symptom of spiritual disorder in the culture.[35] Tate held it absurd to think that all experience could be ordered scientifically; nevertheless, he observed, the tendency to think it could be so ordered had even invaded literary scholarship, where too often method was substituted for intelligence: "The function of criticism should have been in our time, as in all times, to maintain and to demonstrate the special, unique, and complete knowledge which the great forms of literature afford us." [36]

Tate did not manage to define this special knowledge precisely, perhaps because the very nature of such knowledge prevents it; instead, in a series of criticisms of various writers, he illuminated specific poems by approaching their work through technique. Perhaps that is all that can be done, if the knowledge that each poem affords is unique, untranslatable and immanent in the poem itself, as the New Critics have held. Blackmur sardonically

[34] Blackmur, "Toward a Modus Vivendi," *ibid.,* p. 6.
[35] Allen Tate, "The Present Function of Criticism" in *On the Limits of Poetry* (New York: Morrow, 1948).
[36] *Ibid.,* p. 8.

observed in one of his essays, "Criticism, even more than scholar-ship, was a regrettable necessity in the first place." [37] Literature, according to this view, presents life formalized, so that it can be contemplated. Criticism should lead us to the fullest contemplation and to the ability to discriminate among worthy and unworthy formalizations.

Perhaps a little more can be said about the sort of knowledge available to us from the antiscientific, antiphilosophical, anti-conceptual form which these critics held to be literature. In order to face this matter it is well to pause momentarily to summarize our findings and then to proceed to a brief elucidation of some philosophical principles underlying various attitudes of the New Criticism and certain influential later critics.

By backing and filling, by negation and occasional affirmation, criticism came to this point some time in the first half of the twentieth century: It held that poetic language or language in poetry is not essentially referential. It is more inclined to be contextual, that is, dependent for its meaning on the total coherence of the poem, each part being affected by the pressure of the whole. On the other hand, discursive language is primarily referential. Poetry is free from scientific verification of its assertions and from finding things in nature to which its discrete words or statements must correspond. Poetry allows for ambiguity, emphasizes unity, and asserts that each poem generates, on the analogy of an organism, its own unique order.

However, this argument does not show that other forms of discourse may not also operate according to a principle of coherence. If it were possible to do so, then the claim that the poem gives us knowledge while remaining contextual and autonomous would be a stronger one. Clearly, logical discourse has a principle of coherence, namely logic itself, within which lies the assumption that all tropes are properly employed only for illustrative or rhetorical purposes and are therefore secondary to the logical structure itself. One of the principles of logical discourse is that language is primarily referential. One difference between poetry and logical discourse would seem to be that the same logical principles apply generally to all forms claiming logic, while poetic coherence takes as many forms as there are coherent poems. Each poem generates its own order. One of the principles of poetic discourse is that it is not referential. To repeat: The conclusion is that there is one set of laws external to each logical discourse to which each discourse must conform.

[37] Blackmur, "The Lion and the Honeycomb," in Blackmur, *op. cit.*, p. 184.

There is no external set of laws to which each poem must conform—except, of course, that it must be composed of language. But there is a principle that each poem must create its own unique order.

We can speculate further that generalizations can be made about groups of poems—that they act in this or that way, that they have these or those characteristics. The fundamental principle of unique organicism does not and should not prevent us from observing common properties. A way of achieving a unique order may be similar to another way without the products being the same. In examining the ways poems achieve uniqueness it should always be possible to show how these ways prevent the separation of form from content and the substitution of paraphrase for poem.

What fundamental ideas underlie these views? There is perhaps a hint of them in Blackmur's remark that the literary critic is interested in the "ulterior techniques of conceptual form and of symbolic form." [38] The term "symbolic form" has a more general meaning in Ernst Cassirer's formulation than in Blackmur's. Blackmur and the New Criticism could have found in Cassirer's particular extensions and developments of Kantian insights some considerable sanction for their views of the autonomy of the poem. In trying to develop a "philosophy of human culture," Cassirer concluded that man should be defined in terms of his cultural activities, as a maker of language, myth, science, religion, art, and history. He termed each of these cultural creations a "symbolic form" and concluded that rather than defining man as an *animal rationale* we should call him an *animal symbolicum*.[39] Man has surrounded himself with language and other cultural forms to the extent that he cannot see anything without these forms as media. Rather than inhabiting a world of things, he inhabits a world of symbolic reality. There is no hope of escaping symbolization. Practically speaking, there is no reality worth the name apart from man's symbolizings. Kant's limitation was that he posited only one symbolic form and its categories—that of the understanding. He limited knowledge to the scientific concepts built up by the understanding.

Cassirer's idea of symbolism is quite different from the Romantic one exemplified by Carlyle, which insists on the infinite figured forth in finite forms. To Cassirer the infinite and things in

---

[38] Blackmur, "A Burden for Critics," *ibid.*, p. 210.
[39] Ernst Cassirer, *An Essay on Man* (New Haven, Conn.: Yale Univ. Press, 1944), p. 26.

themselves are not of interest, for we cannot know them even through art. What is important is the variety of symbolic forms themselves and their respective inner principles of order. The two primordial symbolic forms are language and myth. In the past a variety of explanations of myth have attempted to reduce it to some alien principle. There have been the allegorical interpreters, the Freudians, the sun theorists, the moon theorists, and so forth. According to Cassirer, all fail to observe myth on its own terms. All reduce it to some intellectual principle alien to its inherent formal structures. Examined from within, myth proves to have an order of its own. It is not a crude form of science. It exists among those who have a considerable practical sense. Mythic expressions cannot be judged as if they are crude empirical statements or allegories behind which lie such statements. Myth is synthetic, not analytic. It insists by the principles of its own coherence on the solidarity of all things:

> Primitive man by no means lacks the ability to grasp the em-
> pirical differences of things. But in his conception of nature and
> life all these differences are obliterated by a stronger feeling: the
> deep conviction of a fundamental and indelible *solidarity of life*
> that bridges over the multiplicity and variety of its single forms.[40]

In mythical thinking, unity and organicism dominate. Mythic metamorphosis emphasizes the oneness of things. No limits are set to time and space. All things are alive; death is an accident.

Language and myth apparently arose together. The various theories of the origin of language have not satisfactorily expressed its nature. The theories that language arose from onomatopoeia or sheer interjection have not shown us how man got from the interjection to the proposition. A structural approach is perhaps more revealing. Phonetics and semantics cannot be kept separate. Cassirer's view is that language is in some way constitutive of our reality. Until the child forms concepts by naming he is lost in the manifold of sensation. Our everyday language is vague and incapable of passing the rigid test of logic, but even so it is a step on the road to scientific concepts and a theoretical view of the world.

In his analysis of language Cassirer seems to be assuming that its only direction is toward scientific symbolization. After establishing a clear relation between the development of language and mythical thinking and after presenting an analysis of myth that makes us think at once of literature, Cassirer fails somehow to

[40] *Ibid.*, p. 82.

follow out the implications of his remarks for literary theory. When he turns to art he does not discuss literary art as specifically an art of language. He does not see language as developing both toward scientific and literary symbolic forms, with science rejecting and literature embracing the unifying principle of mythical thinking purged of its demand for literal belief.

Yet Cassirer's discussion of art *does* constantly use literary examples. He sees theories of art fluctuating historically between objective and subjective poles. On the one hand there are theories of imitation, which parallel the onomatopoetic theories of the origin of language. There is considerable uneasiness in these theories about admitting so-called improvements on nature, for these improvements seem to violate the laws of "truth." On the other hand there are expressive theories, which parallel the interjection theories of language. Cassirer argues that although art surely expresses, it is surely also formative. He insists that the artist is not absorbed in his own pleasure or grief but in contemplation and creation of specific forms of expression.

It seems at this point that Cassirer's interest would move logically to the specific forms, to the media of the artist. But such is not the case. Cassirer seems to ignore the fact that there is a linguistic art and again associates language purely with science:

> Language and science are abbreviations of reality; art is an intensification of reality. Language and science depend upon one and the same process of abstraction; art may be described as a continuous process of concretion . . . . art does not admit of . . . conceptual simplification and deductive generalization . . . . The artist is just as much a discoverer of the forms of nature as the scientist is a discoverer of facts or natural laws.[41]

We pay a high price for our abstracting intellective powers, because such abstraction is always an "impoverishment of reality." Things tend to be reduced in scientific symbolizations to formulae of ultimate simplicity, and we are sometimes tempted to think that all of reality is available to us reduced in this way. But we are wrong, "For the aspects of things are innumerable, and they vary from one moment to another. Any attempt to comprehend them within a simple formula would be in vain." [42] Art, then, is in a symbolic form life actually lived. Art intensifies rather than abbreviates reality. It does this not according to the laws of empirical science or with reference to an exterior object

[41] *Ibid.*, pp. 143–44.
[42] *Ibid.*, p. 144.

it somehow represents, but according to a principle of artistic coherence.

At this point Cassirer finally associates art with myth. The poet and the mythmaker are, as Giambattista Vico observed, endowed with an identical fundamental power of personification. The difference between art and myth is that mythical thought contains an element of naive literal belief, while the artist releases his forms from this necessity. This is not to deny that the work of art conveys knowledge. It is to say that the knowledge it conveys it conveys as a total form, not as a group of parts each of which is established as referring to something real on the outside. One reason for this is that the so-called outside world no longer exists simply out there in the way the naive primitive mythmaker believes it to exist. By the same token, the outside world posited by the symbolic form of science is only a creation of *that* symbolic form, and the principle of verification is only a principle applicable within that form. The world of science is out there only because the symbolic form of science creates the coherent fiction of its otherness.

Cassirer presents an analysis of the development of Romantic criticism similar to that presented early in this chapter. Romantic criticism quite properly developed a theory of imagination and gave a constitutive power to poetry, the product of imagination, but in practice it went off base by confusing the transcendent with the symbolic. The result was entrapment of the poem in conceptual generalizations. Oddly enough the naturalists and realists, who denied the epistemology leading to the idea of symbolic forms, concentrated on particularity in their art, erroneously defending their practice with a positivism that considered science the only way to truth. We see, from the point of view we are describing, the Romantics with the right theory and the wrong practice and the naturalists with the right practice and the wrong theory. Cassirer points out that art is symbolic but symbolism in art must be associated with the particular and immanent and not the general and transcendent. The metaphysical infinite is not the end art seeks: "It is to be sought in certain fundamental structural elements of our sense experience —in lines, design, in architectural, musical forms." [43] The physical world is not a "bundle of sense-data," and the world of art is not a bundle of feelings and emotions. Art proceeds to immediate appearances and their forms; it is interested in the multiplicity of life as it is experienced.

[43] *Ibid.*, p. 157.

All of this seems related somehow to ideas of variety and complexity in Richards and in Brooks. It reminds one of Croce's idea that intuitions are actually made in expression. Cassirer's shortcoming is his failure to analyze specifically the artistic use of language as against the scientific or abstracting use. He has thus ignored the medium even as he has seemed to imply that the medium is everything. His approach to art is first concerned with the artist's activity, but it holds forth the possibility of an objective principle. It insists that art can give knowledge without the necessity of submitting its statements individually to canons of verification. The reason is that the symbolic form of art does not make statements as detachable statements but as part of a total form that generates its own laws. We cannot judge what it does say or, perhaps better, what it is by the alien standards of some other symbolic form.

But Cassirer does not, any more than Croce, give us the attention to the medium that his own position must ultimately insist upon. In fact, Cassirer never actually asserts that there is an art which takes language to a destination other than that of formulating concepts unambiguously.

Perhaps he takes us far enough, however, so that we can see the difference between "meaning" and "being" as these words apply to literature considered as a symbolic form. In a sense any symbolization belonging to any symbolic form "means," but there is also a stricter sense in which it can only mean itself. This is theoretically true in science and absolutely true in art; because the principle of art we have been discussing insists on the unique structure of each work. There is nothing behind it or out there to which it is supposed to refer or by which its statements can be verified. In this sense it *means* only what it *is,* and therefore it has *being* rather than *meaning.* Behind or beyond the work is only the manifold of sensation, which is nothing until given form by the completed artistic act. That act is imagination, intuition, expression, and externalization all rolled into one.

There is also a sense in which scientific forms have only being. Behind them too is only the manifold. But scientific forms insist as a principle of their structure on hypothesizing the "objective" reality of something beyond them that can be known. They insist on referentiality as a sort of category of their symbolism. From a purely detached point of view it would be necessary to call this recourse to the external a fiction created by the scientific symbolic form. When we step into this symbolism and think in its categories, we willingly suspend our theoretical disbelief and accept the fiction that conceptual language "means" or refers to something. In another more Olympian sense, however, we can say that the resulting conceptualizations have only "being." This becomes clearer when we consider "the pride of human reason," mathematics, that is totally abstract and nonreferential although it is employed by the symbolic form of science to build up ideas of external reality.

In considering this whole matter we have perhaps come to recognize that a critical approach via technique like that advocated by Blackmur seems inevitable to a criticism working out of these ideas. These ideas imply that the formal constructions of language and other symbols totally regulate content, for the content (if that is what it may be called, for it is not separable) *is* the formal structure. We recognize at last Archibald MacLeish's point when he insists in his famous poem "Ars Poetica" that a poem should not mean but be.

# 6 RECENT CONSIDERATIONS

The polemics of the New Criticism were met in academia by the violent antipathy of vested interests. Nothing could have been further from the concerns exhibited by the historicism or the philological studies that formed the center—the still center, the New Critics might have quipped—of the typical English department in an American university. The state of those departments at that time can be explained by the historical fact that literature as a subject of study had entered academia in a very oblique way.[1] Originally literature was attached to the study of language, and at first to only Greek and Latin. The literatures of these languages were studied primarily because the works were examples of Greek and Latin, not because they were literature, although of course the classic authors were held in the greatest respect. English entered the curriculum by analogy as a philological discipline. As with the pattern followed in respect to Greek and Latin, the dead languages of Old and Middle English were studied through such specimens as *Beowulf* and *The Canterbury Tales*. Modern English literature from the Renaissance up to but probably not including William Wordsworth struggled to enter a curriculum already ruled by philological interest. It crashed through because the philological orientation was gradually broadening to include cultural history.

[1] An interesting discussion of this and related matters occurs in Walter J. Ong, "Synchronic Present: The Academic Future of Modern Literature in America," *Approaches to the Study of Twentieth-Century Literature,* Proceedings of the Conference in the Study of Twentieth-Century Literature, 1st Session (East Lansing: Michigan State Univ. Press, 1961), pp. 55–76.

That later literature, including American, only slowly gained admission to the curriculum was probably the result of the philological bias operating irrationally even as its originally linguistic emphasis was dying. Somehow the idea persisted that a language had to be dead to be studied. By a curious analogy, then, so did a literature. The historical emphasis that replaced the linguistic was convenient because it could easily adopt the same antiquarianism, history being about the past. The development of the teaching of American literature is instructive in this matter, because of its conservatism. Teachers of American literature became, by and large, intellectual historians, because at the time they sought admission to the academy, historical scholarship was the most respectable mode of literary study. Even today the study of American literature remains less oriented to modern critical developments than does the study of English literature.

New Critics like Allen Tate did not tire of pointing out that the methods of philology and historicism were the methods of positivism, a philosophy with no interest in art. The cultural historian might make judgments for or against poets on any number of grounds—economic, political, sociological—but he was not concerned with artistic values or art's unique function.

The movements of the late nineteenth century in France and England, known sometimes as aestheticism and sometimes as art for art's sake, may be seen as an effort to assert art's own particular character and purpose, but since "purpose" and "use" had been successfully appropriated by positivism, the aesthetes were pleased to assert the "uselessness" of art. Aestheticism failed to develop a really viable aesthetic theory but influenced all later criticism. When the New Critics appeared, the philologists and cultural historians, in their own positivism, assumed that the New Critics were merely the aesthetes again. Besides, several of these critics were professed poets. Poets had not been thought to belong properly in English departments.

That is perhaps unnecessarily sarcastic, but sarcasm is at least true to the tone of the debate that raged in academia during the forties. Woe to the young graduate student caught in the crossfire! The matter comes up for mention here because the intellectual aims of the New Critics during this time were so often misconceived. The New Critics were not, as many of the cultural historians seemed to think, trying to separate literature from life. Their view was that philological and historical scholarship had made literature disappear by converting it into linguistic specimen or historical document. The critic should read literature as if it were an art. This meant literature had to be distinguished from other modes of statement conceptual in nature and subject to rational standards or proof. The New Critics held that poetry was a mode of language with its own unique cultural value; it returned man from the abstractions of intellect to a contemplation of the particulars and complexities of individual experience.

A new pedagogical method, first formally espoused in Cleanth Brooks and Robert Penn Warren's *Understanding Poetry*, won a victory in academia, though here and there bands of defenders held out even after the war had ended, sometimes out of ignorance of events. The teaching of literature was fundamentally changed by these events; it has not and will not return to its former state. But, of course, with victory, the revolutionary fervor subsided and a period of reconsideration and perhaps stultification followed. There is no perfection in criticism, no final word. Theoreticians continue to puzzle over new difficulties bestowed by the latest advances in the subject. In the wake or across the wake of the New Criticism has come a variety of developments, some of which will be mentioned in this chapter.

The contextualist emphasis of the New Criticism is still subjected to attacks by those who accuse it of attempting to remove poetry from life. Others attack it still for its supposedly conservative or even fascistic political implications. We shall not be detained by the latter complaint, which is principally *ad hominem*. The former is more fundamental and requires examination, however, because it is based on a popular epistemology that thoughtlessly assumes that language is always referential, always points beyond itself to objects, and always offers its propositions for verification. The view that the poem is autonomous and self-enclosed seems to imply to someone holding this simple assumption that the poem is unrelated to other human concerns. This the New Critics would vehemently deny. A careful reading of Tate shows that if he cut the poem off from our everyday concerns in theory (and I doubt this is so), in practice he was deeply concerned with literature's relation to life. To some extent the problem is that the writings of Tate and of John Crowe Ransom, which come nearest to providing a theoretical base for contextualist criticism, are lacking in philosophical rigor and semantic clarity. Murray Krieger's *The New Apologists for Poetry*, a discussion of the theoretical implications of the critical movement from Hulme and Eliot through Richards to Ransom, Tate, and

Brooks, leaves one impressed with the continuity of the interests of the New Criticism but convinced that its philosophical position—fundamentally its epistemology—was not fully expressed.

Perhaps it is for this reason that attacks have continued on about the same level of sophistication as years before. Rather than arguing the epistemological issue, the point is simply repeated that the contextualists separate the poem from its referents or "life," that they are the nineteenth-century aesthetes again. An attack by Walter Sutton in two articles appearing in 1958 and 1961 argues that if the poem is autonomous and contextual, it cannot appeal to common experience.[2] Sutton believes that the contextualist critic seals off the realm of art as "a kind of haven (or heaven) of unremitting pleasure and gratification, affording an escape from the conflict and tension of ordinary life." Sutton's attack seemed to be pointed particularly at the theorizing of Eliseo Vivas.

Both Vivas and his defender Krieger replied, trying to clarify the arguments Vivas had previously made in his book *Creation and Discovery*. They claimed that Sutton had attributed false views to the contextualists and then proceeded to attack them.[3] No modern contextualist held that poetry was an escape. Indeed, as "The Affective Fallacy" of Wimsatt and Beardsley shows, the contextualists vehemently and consistently attacked the very sort of aesthetic hedonism and escapism that Sutton had attributed to them. They insisted that the idea of contextual meaning did not suggest that the contextual critics believed the reader did not bring his own experience to bear upon the poem. No one in his right mind had ever doubted that the reader brings his common experience to the poem. Vivas argued, however (after asking just what reader we are talking about), that the poem tests the reader's experience, not vice versa. The question is whether the poem has the power of persuasion in itself, not simply whether it endorses the reader's already formulated and accepted attitudes and feelings. Krieger added:

[2] Walter Sutton, "The Contextualist Dilemma—or Fallacy?" *Journal of Aesthetics and Art Criticism*, Vol. 17, No. 2 (December 1958), pp. 219–29; "Contextualist Theory and Criticism as a Social Act," *Journal of Aesthetics and Art Criticism*, Vol. 19, No. 3 (Spring 1961), pp. 317–25.

[3] See Eliseo Vivas, *Creation and Discovery* (New York: Noonday, 1955), also *The Artistic Transaction* (Columbus: Ohio State Univ. Press, 1963). Vivas' reply to Sutton's first article is reprinted in the latter volume, pp. 171–202, and titled "Contextualism Reconsidered." Krieger's reply, "Contextualism Was Ambitious," appeared in *Journal of Aesthetics and Art Criticism*, Vol. 21, No. 1 (Fall 1962), pp. 81–88.

I like to think the critic [and I suppose he would also mean any reader] is less than the poem, that he learns from it instead of demanding that it tell him what he has known from elsewhere, demanding that it relate experiences similar to those he has had or understands, in short that it become a projection of himself that can be measured by himself.[4]

Vivas got to the bottom of the matter by arguing that Sutton's disagreement with him, never clearly stated, was over the nature of language. Sutton seemed to be holding that language is always primarily referential. Vivas argued that poetic language is fundamentally "constitutive." The poet does not merely manipulate words each with its own discrete referentiality, nor does he make an assertion to be tested by methods of verification. Instead, he makes "constitutive symbols" that create and shape reality *in* the linguistic utterance itself. Vivas expressed annoyance that anyone could possibly conclude that his theoretical stance separated art from life or from everyday experience when his whole effort had been to insist that "art plays a constitutive role in the rest of life, and the rest of life offers itself to art as a matter to be transubstanced into the substance of art." [5] By this he meant that in any culture there are many values and meanings "imbedded and . . . inchoately realized" if they are consciously realized at all, for they are not "constituted" in any symbolic form. These values and meanings, as yet in a sense unreal, are "knocking at the gate of history," as it were. The poet "discovers" their true nature by "creating" these objects linguistically, as other kinds of artists create and discover in other media. Once the poem is made, the meanings are real, shaped; they are their form, where before they were merely vague intimations of the manifold of sensation. In Vivas's language, those objects that have previously "subsisted" only vaguely in the culture now "insist" in the poem, indeed *as* the poem. Then comes the inevitable abstraction of meaning and value out of the poetic context. Actually the real, full meanings and values cannot be abstracted because they are the poem itself. But the abstraction nevertheless takes place, at the expense of loss. Values are then isolated from the poem and meanings are "institutionalized in men's actions"; in other words, they now "exist."

When this takes place they are no longer dependent on the language in which the poet revealed them, and ostensive language

[4] Krieger, *op cit.*, p. 85.
[5] Vivas, *The Artistic Transaction,* p. 7.

can now refer to them. We can speak of Trojan horse tactics, of a man's quixotism; we speak of a man we know as a Don Juan or a Hamlet . . . .[6]

In one sense, these meanings, torn from the poem, are a gain for society; but in another sense they are diminished from their original being in or as the poem. We must return to Homer to know the real meaning of the Trojan horse. This is, of course, a very simple example of an idea having much more complex application.

It is interesting to consider Vivas' theory in the light of the argument that concludes Shelley's famous *Defence of Poetry* (1821):

> Poets are the hierophants of an unapprehended inspiration; the mirrors of the gigantic shadows which futurity casts upon the present; the words which express what they understand not; the trumpets which sing to battle, and feel not what they inspire; the influence which is moved not, but moves. Poets are the unacknowledged legislators of the world.

Shelley was less concerned with the medium than Vivas, but both seem to be insisting on similar cultural functions for poetry.

Once values and meanings torn from poems are institutionalized, Vivas' work reminds us, readers get the impression that the poem imitates meanings and values that somehow they have been aware of all along. But this is an illusion. One thinks of Ernst Cassirer's discussion of how Helen Keller suddenly entered the world of verbal symbolism when her teacher held her hand under a faucet and tapped out the code for "water." Although she had of course experienced water, in an important sense she had not, until it had been fixed or "constituted" by the word. None of us remembers when we did not have words and know things; we tend to think that we always did.

The poet who merely imitates objects already fully realized in the culture is not a poet of consequence, for he is merely reporting instead of making "constitutive" symbols. Vivas includes, no doubt, among the lesser breed of poets the writer who caters to those pleasant or nostalgic experiences with which the reader already feels safe, playing upon his likely sentimentalism in response to recognizable values. One can readily understand from this analysis the artistic difficulties of being poet

[6] Vivas, *Creation and Discovery*, p. 139.

laureate. We might conclude from Vivas' argument that the good poet is not always welcome in society, particularly if he brings to the surface and offers for "existence" attitudes vaguely possessed without acknowledgment by the culture. The poet A. J. M. Smith has remarked that the poet is a tattletale, a peeping Tom. He is suggesting a function consistent with Vivas' theory. We see also that in a conservative state like Plato's commonwealth the poet is a potentially dangerous influence because he is making new material for ideas. Tolerance of poets is probably in inverse proportion to the totalitarian nature of any society.

Vivas' contextualism, which is an extension into theory of New Critical practice and is also heavily in the debt of Cassirer, emphasizes the cultural significance of literature. In Vivas' view, it would seem that good art insists on making society know itself, while bad art, because it "constitutes" nothing, invites society to remain content with its illusions.

A similar view is promulgated in Herbert Read's book on art, *Icon and Idea*. There the argument goes that in human culture the idea is not only preceded by but also derived from the icon. We can never move from a pre-ideational form of knowing to a totally ideational life. For new ideas to be created, new icons must be created. We can never become the enlightenment's ideal, the pure *animal rationale,* and divest ourselves of icon-making. Throughout history the *animal rationale* must ride piggyback on the *animal symbolicum*.

According to Vivas, no one doubts that each of us brings his experience to art. We must know what a poem's words mean. But art is supposed to give us more than we bring to it. Even though it may puzzle us at first or second glance, its aim is to arouse, in Vivas' words, "an aesthetic experience of rapt attention which involves the intransitive apprehension of an object's immanent meanings and values in their full presentational immediacy." [7] By "intransitive" Vivas means that "attention is aesthetic when it is so controlled by the object that it does not fly away from it to meanings and values not present immanently in the object . . . ." [8] These definitions clearly take us back to Immanuel Kant and to Samuel Taylor Coleridge's "willing suspension of disbelief"; they even are distant cousins of Richards' balance of impulses. The reader of literature is not considered

[7] Vivas, *The Artistic Transaction,* p. 30.
[8] Vivas, *Creation and Discovery,* p. 96.

the recipient of a conceptual statement. Instead he is to focus his attention on the "structural richness of the composition." He accepts the universe of the poem.

Of course, there are myriad responses possible to any object; and there are aesthetic responses to things other than artistic objects. Vivas points out, however, that we recognize only the art object as a design to evoke "intransitive rapt attention." As readers we must be prepared to learn to exercise such attention where it is warranted. To insist on reading Dante transitively is to become involved in conceptual problems. Is Hell really down in the earth with Satan at its center? Such a question should not arise if Dante's poem is a success and if we have really learned to read poems.

The argument of Cleanth Brooks against some of Shelley's poems implies that even if we come to them prepared they insist in themselves on our treating some of their statements as detachable concepts. The concepts too openly obtrude upon the reader. The real complaint of Richards against his students was that they could not achieve intransitive attention no matter how accessible to intransitivity the poem actually was. It is important to notice that Vivas' affective interests are dissolved back into an interest in the structure of the object. In keeping the eye on the object, one tries to avoid all the difficulties implicit in locating the poem in the reader's response.

Side by side with a contextualist criticism associated closely with modern aesthetics—the criticism we have been concerned with in Chapter 5 and in the last few pages—there developed in this century a mode of criticism closely associated with modern anthropology and mythography. One historian of this movement traces its genesis to Charles Darwin's *Origin of Species,* which suggested the possibility of a "variety of genetic studies of culture." [9] A more specific landmark is the work of the Cambridge school of anthropologists, especially that of James G. Frazer (*The Golden Bough*) and Jane Ellen Harrison (*Prolegomena to*

[9] Stanley Edgar Hyman, "The Ritual View and the Mythic" in T. A. Sebeok, ed., *Myth: A Symposium* (Bloomington: Indiana Univ. Press, 1958), pp. 84–94. Reprinted in John B. Vickery, ed., *Myth and Literature* (Lincoln, Nebraska: Univ. of Nebraska Press, 1966), pp. 47–58. Hyman's essay is in effect a valuable bibliography of the development of the subject. Other symposia on myth are Bernice Slote, ed., *Myth and Symbol* (Lincoln: Univ. of Nebraska Press, 1963), H. A. Murray, ed., *Myth and Myth-Making* (New York: Braziller, 1960).

*the Study of Greek Religion.*)[10] These books were followed by studies of the mythic and ritualistic origins of Greek tragedy and ultimately by the treatment of mythic patterns in later literature.[11] At the same time contemporary writers of poems, novels, and plays employed these patterns and motifs self-consciously in their own works.

Parallel to the developments in anthropology were those researches of Sigmund Freud and his followers that gradually revealed links between myths and dreams and created new rubrics for commentators as well as poets.[12] It became fashionable to interpret literary works as myths or as dreams, to discover either in the foreground of, or submerged in, a literary work an ancient ritual as reconstructed by Frazer or Harrison or Weston or a dream pattern as analyzed by Freud or Jung.

What did the existence of these patterns mean? Was literature simply a form for the retelling of these old stories? Was it merely the externalization of dreams? Unsophisticated commentary tended simply to reduce complex literary structures to mythic patterns, overlooking the idea of the uniqueness and autonomy of the work so painstakingly insisted upon by the contextualists. The poem was often viewed as an imitation of the one eternal symbolic pattern, repeatable in endless variations through literature and art, myth and dream.

Yet it could not be denied that the analogies discovered among literary works, dreams, and myths were striking and not to be disregarded. It was not remembered by all, however, that the artist still had to deal with a medium and that if he dreamed, he was surely awake when he wrote. The work of Cassirer is useful in helping us to illustrate the importance of recognizing the differences and similarities between myths and art. As we have seen, Cassirer examined myth not as a story or congeries of stories but as a *way* of thought and expression, a primitive means of constituting reality. He saw language and myth as a twin birth, with language moving toward emancipation of itself from mythical categories to those of science. Although he acknowl-

---

[10] Also by Frazer, *Folk-lore in the Old Testament* (1918), *The Worship of Nature* (1926). Also by Harrison, *Themis* (1912), *Ancient Art and Ritual* (1913), and *Epilegomena to the Study of Greek Religion* (1921).

[11] See especially Gilbert Murray's *The Rise of the Greek Epic* (1907), his "Hamlet and Orestes" in *The Classical Tradition in Poetry* (1927), and Jessie L. Weston's *From Ritual to Romance* (1920).

[12] The major work is perhaps Freud's *Totem and Taboo* (1913).

edged a symbolic form called art, he did not explicitly relate myth and literature except by analogy. Yet it is clear that with a little extension we can see his mythic categories present in literary art, purged of the element of naive referential belief they possessed in primitive culture. Cassirer insisted finally that art was its own universe of discourse.

By the 1950's almost in spite of itself the New Criticism and its contextualism had spawned a new sort of scholarship replacing the old historical positivism attacked by Tate. This scholarship, which had seized on the methods implied in the theory and practice particularly of such critics as Brooks and Warren, interested itself almost exclusively in the interior relationships among the parts of the poem. Mainly because of what it left out it invited the attacks of the sort leveled against it by Sutton. Its method had abandoned the cultural interests out of which the method had originally come. The theoretical work of Vivas was one effort to escape from the domination of method and to establish the cultural importance of literature in contextual terms; he did not neglect to admit that he had stolen as much as he could from Cassirer. He had not, however, examined all the possibilities of myth.

This was being done by Northrop Frye in the most influential body of critical theory since the New Critics. Frye's work began with a study of William Blake called *Fearful Symmetry* (1947), in which the outlines of a theoretical approach were traceable. Working in a neo-Blakean fashion, adopting something like Cassirer's idea of symbolic forms, heavily in the debt of modern anthropology, appropriating insights from Freud and Jung, and returning to the language and some of the methodology of Aristotle, he produced in 1957 his *Anatomy of Criticism,* an effort to consolidate the gains of contextualism with myth and ritual study.[13] Frye sought to preserve the idea of literature im-

[13] This view that Frye sought to synthesize contextualism and myth and ritual studies is not held by all of Frye's critics, some of whom consider him an utter alternative to the modern critical tradition. See Murray Krieger, ed., *Northrop Frye in Modern Criticism* (New York: Columbia Univ. Press, 1966), especially the introduction. The book includes essays on Frye by Geoffrey H. Hartman, Angus Fletcher, and W. K. Wimsatt, with Frye's reply. The title *Anatomy of Criticism* has a sort of irony in it, as befits Frye's belief that we are in an ironic age of literature. One of the genres that Frye isolates for discussion is the "anatomy," a literary work which is a form of prose fiction containing a "great variety of subject-matter and a strong interest in ideas." Its author's method is characterized by "piling up an enormous mass of erudition about his theme or in overwhelming his pedantic targets with an avalanche of their own jargon."

plicit in the contextualists' principle of autonomy, but he employed the study of archetypes to follow its implications into a consideration of literature as hypothetically a total form. The suggestion was that literature makes up part of a larger cultural totality and performs an ethical function.

Frye begins with complaints about the state that criticism has been in ever since Aristotle's valiant effort to make something reasonably systematic of it. He likes Aristotle because Aristotle named things. As far as he can see, no one has managed to step significantly beyond or even to carry out the principles implied by Aristotle's systematic approach. Later we recognize that Frye does not really consider all criticism since Aristotle hopeless. He himself is greatly influenced by Eliot and by the Romantic principles of organism. He even finds a contextualist principle in Aristotle's theory of imitation.

Frye argues in his "Polemical Introduction" to *Anatomy of Criticism* that criticism must have its own conceptual framework and this framework must be derived from an inductive study of literature itself. It must not be borrowed, as so often in the past, from some other discipline. In insisting, to this extent, that criticism become scientific, he is well aware of the red flag he has raised; but that, of course, is half the fun. He takes his chances with the superficial reader for whom the cherished difference between literature and science is somehow endangered if criticism is not kept totally unscientific. Frye believes that this antiscientism in criticism has contributed to the continued chaos of critical method. Criticism, according to Frye, remains in the state of "naive induction" from which Aristotle tried to rescue it. It is like chemistry previous to its emancipation from alchemy, that is, the *materials* of literature are somehow thought to constitute the *structure* of criticism instead of being "phenomena to be explained in terms of a conceptual framework." Just as in physics we do not learn nature, but physics, so in literary criticism we study criticism, not literature. Literature, like nature, is an object of study, not a subject, and can therefore only be directly experienced, neither taught nor learned.

---

Frye argues that criticism must develop scientific procedures, but the title is a reminder that criticism is also an art. One reviewer, Frank Kermode, has called Frye's book useless like art. I suspect that in calling his book an anatomy Frye anticipated that the ideas *insisting* in his book would come to *existence* outside the book in a rather thinned condition. Books by Frye subsequent to *Anatomy of Criticism* are *Fables of Identity,* a collection of essays, *The Well-Tempered Critic, The Educated Imagination, The Modern Century,* and collected essays on Milton and Shakespeare.

Every conceptual framework must have a central hypothesis. Frye holds that just as we assume there is an order of nature behind the natural sciences, we must assume an order of words behind literary criticism, not merely a huge stretch of discrete works arranged from Homer onward, elongating with each latest novel. Having said this, he is quick to acknowledge the claims of contextualism: Poetry is a "disembodied use of words." In other words, it is contextual. It is contrasted to descriptive or assertive writing that has something to *say*. Frye characterizes the difference with the words "centrifugal" and "centripetal." The reader begins reading a poem with the hypothesis that it is a centripetally organized unity. Even when literature is heavily influenced by descriptive or didactic centrifugal principles, as in the documentary naturalism of Zola or Dreiser, it is still centripetal. The best example of rigorous self-conscious centripetality is French *Symbolisme*. Frye draws an analogy between literature and mathematics: The poet, like the mathematician, depends not on descriptive truth but on "conformity to his hypothetical postulates."

Nevertheless, Frye insists on maintaining the idea of imitation, hoping to purify it of the naively referential meaning accreted to it after Aristotle, and using it as he assumes Aristotle meant it. To some, this adherence to imitation has been vaguely like Richards using Coleridge's idealistic terminology in a materialistic argument,[14] but one can perhaps distinguish the two strategies by observing that Richards' materialism could not clarify but only obfuscate Coleridge's ideas, while Frye's principle of symbolic form may possibly clarify Aristotle's *mimesis* and complete his thought. At any rate, Frye interprets *mimesis*

> not as a Platonic "recollection" but as an emancipation of externality into image, nature into art. From this point of view the work of art must be its own object: it cannot be ultimately descriptive of something, and can never be ultimately related to any other system of phenomena, standards, values, or final causes.[15]

Frye seems to mean by imitation something similar to what Vivas means by the transformation of subsistence into poetic insistence. He may be close to R. S. Crane's formulation in *The Language of Criticism and the Structure of Poetry,* to be discussed shortly, in which the object of *mimesis* is actually created by the poem. Thus a poem imitates the action it creates. Frye perhaps is

[14] *Coleridge on Imagination* (New York: Norton, 1950).
[15] *Anatomy of Criticism* (Princeton, N.J.: Princeton Univ. Press, 1957), p. 113.

joining Aristotelian terminology to the constitutive principle of Cassirer. In Aristotelian *mimesis,* Frye argues, the poem does not represent or reflect external events or ideas (it is not centrifugal); instead, it exists between the example and the precept. Example and precept are meant to recall Aristotle's placing of poetry between history and moral philosophy. Since both example and precept imply centrifugality, and it is hard to see how something between the two would not imply it, perhaps it is at this point that Frye might have emancipated himself from Aristotle. He is in danger of falling abruptly, as was Aristotle, into the idea of a separable content to be conveyed. He attempts to extricate himself by insisting that the ideas of literature are not real propositions but verbal formulas that imitate real propositions. They are, that is, parts of a centripetal whole in which the propositions contained therein are totally emancipated from their usefulness or verifiability or whatever in them is external to the poem. They become part of the image. Perhaps here finally after several centuries we have a subtle expansion of what Jacopo Mazzoni had to say about the idol.

When we offer a commentary upon a poem, which has been constructed as an object rather than by an alignment of words with meanings or referents, we produce a form of allegorical interpretation because we are translating what is implicit in the poem into the explicitness of commentary. Such commentary is usually tied to the particular interests and vocabularies of a time and place. In order to transcend the tendency of each most recent and fashionable discipline to convert the poem to its terms and purposes, literary criticism needs a hypothesis of its own, which presumably would lead to an autonomous critical language. This does not mean that literature is unrelated to other systems of symbolism. It can "enter into any kind of relationship to them," but literature as a system remains a hypothetical creation of criticism. Frye's explanatory analogy is mathematics, a self-enclosed system that enters into relationships with other systems, always on its own terms.

If there is to be a critical hypothesis it must be twofold. To account for the contextualist nature of the poem, it must be assumed that the poem is an artifact with its own structure, an imitation as Frye specifically defines it. (Perhaps "metamorphosis" would be a better word.) It is also related by common properties to other things belonging to literature—that is, in a quite different sense, it is an imitation of other poems. Frye makes much of Pope's lines, remarking that Virgil discovered that following nature and Homer were the same.[16] In order to think about literature at all we must have a concept of it, which entails discovering that which literary works fundamentally have in common.

Frye finds his hypothetical principle in the archetype, which is a symbol—"any unit of any literary structure that can be isolated for critical attention"—that "connects one poem to another and thereby helps to unify and integrate our literary experience." [17] It is, in other words, a convention. Frye explicitly states that he sees no reason to bring in a Jungian explanation of the existence of archetypes; he argues that it is an unnecessary hypothesis that will not make new archetypes appear; nor will denial of it cause conventions in literature to disappear. This is not, of course, to deny the immense influence of Carl Jung and the Cambridge anthropologists on Frye, whose work is unthinkable without them as background.

Frye's archetypes are also not Plato's "ideas," which are assumed to be prior to their copies; Frye would claim that his are inductively hypothesized from specific autonomous poetic contexts. But he goes beyond this simple hypothesization to observe that it is a natural part of reading to expand images into conventional archetypes. This means either that archetypes have more existence than hypothesis alone implies, or (preferably) that the act of reading is a critical act employing unconsciously a hypothesis we should consciously accept as fundamental to criticism. Poets themselves consciously or unconsciously employ the hypothesis, though explicit use of archetypes is not now as common as in a period when Biblical and classical learning were part of every reader's equipment.

Archetypes imply for Frye the hypothesis of a "literary universe" that is self-contained, literature as a total form. It must be noticed that Frye does not insist that literature *has a certain content* but that it *is a form*. One is reminded here of "form" as Cassirer uses it—a way of symbolically constituting the world. The mythic patterns that are projections of this way of constructing the "literary universe" are not the content of literature. The myth of the quest and the cyclic symbolism central to literary forms do not *mean*; they are the molds into which nature is poured, in which it is created, in which it is discovered. Most of *Anatomy of Criticism* is devoted to charting these

[16] Northrop Frye, "Nature and Homer" in *Fables of Identity* (New York: Harcourt, Brace & World, 1963), pp. 39–51.
[17] Frye, *Anatomy of Criticism,* pp. 71–99.

structural principles in literature, just as much of *Fearful Symmetry* was a charting of the principles as they informed the work of Blake.

Frye thus tries to escape the idea that he is creating a sort of Platonic monomyth of which every poem is a naive copy or example. Myth is form, not content. This does not, from Frye's point of view, lead to the old form-content division because each poem displaces myth and reconstitutes it in its own fashion rather than filling up the old form with new content. The center of the literary universe is always "whatever poem we happen to be reading," for the literary universe has a logic of space all its own. Frye seems to be saying that criticism must come to terms with the annoying fact that it is trapped within a discursive logic that is at odds with the antilogic of poetry and that it must be liberal enough to allow that antilogic its prerogatives. One of the principles of poetic form is a spatial paradox that puts the center of things ideally at the circumference of them, that insists that man contain his world rather than be contained by it, that demands that the part is the whole, that the microcosm is interchangeable with the macrocosm. By poetic antilogic the poem is a unique container, shaped by archetypes that pull other poems and their use of these symbols into its own totality; by the logic of discourse the poem is hypothetically perceived as *part* of a larger hypothetical unity or universe called literature, held together by common formal elements and a common way of emancipating nature into art.

Just as for Frye the poem contains life and reality by "imitation," so does the hypothetical literary universe hypothetically contain life and reality in its symbolic form. This larger context for the poem is the source from which the structural principles of literature must be derived, if they are to be derived at all, not from the bodies we call anthropology, history, psychology, and so forth. Frye therefore employs the term "myth" in a special way, emancipating it from anthropology. For Frye, "myth" and "ritual" mean only "an abstract or purely literary world of fictional and thematic design." For example: "The ritual of the killing of the divine king in Frazer, whatever it may be in anthropology, is in literary criticism the demonic or undisplaced radical form of tragic and ironic structures." [18] Or:

> It looks now as though Freud's view of the Oedipus complex were a psychological conception that throws some light on literary

[18] *Ibid.*, p. 148.

criticism. Perhaps we shall eventually decide that we have got it the wrong way around: that what happened was that the myth of Oedipus informed and gave structure to some psychological investigations . . . .[19]

In Frye's usage, "myth" and "ritual" do not have extraliterary meanings. Nor do the literary structures these words point to have meaning in poems. They "insist," and only commentary makes them "subsist" (I am, of course, using Vivas' terms here). If it turns out that no Frazerean divine king had ever been ritually killed, it would make no difference to literary structure as we now have it. Frazer would be useful to the literary critic by a sort of fortunate chance, whatever his value may turn out to be for anthropology, because he hit upon certain structural principles of literature. The same applies to Jung, no matter what the competence of his psychoanalytic procedures is.

I have suggested that for Frye the poem and the hypothetical literary universe contain life and reality by "imitation." Actually, for Frye, they contain more than life or reality as we usually think of these things. Appropriating Aristotle again, Frye sees literature as possibly containing all that is imaginable, all that the mind can make as well as all that it can experience from the so-called outside world—all that can be imagined between the mental limits of "desire" and "repugnance." Thus for Frye, as for Aristotle, literature can present men as better than, the same as, or worse than they are. In defining these limits, Frye introduces what becomes for him literature's potential cultural value: Literature can chart not just that which is but that which it is possible to imagine as culturally desirable and undesirable, the total "dream of man." Literature, then, moves nearly into the realm of the purely imagined and pure form; but only nearly. The circle of literature's formal autonomy is, for Frye, never quite closed; its world is necessarily also the mythical thinker's world of immanent "things." The austere perfection of pure form always eludes art. Art ceases to be art and to do art's job when it becomes mathematical, when its language becomes free of denotation and "pure." There is a greater irony in the conclusion of Frye's *Anatomy,* where he discusses this, than in Cassirer's occasional tendency to suggest that art can release itself fully into the realm of pure form. At least, Frye seems to express his irony more clearly than Cassirer managed to do.

Several complaints have been made against Frye, but two are

[19] *Ibid.,* p. 353.

fundamental. The first one has two sides, one that he isolates literature from life in a universe of its own, the other that he returns us to all the problems implicit in the idea of imitation. The claim of isolation will not hold, any more than will Sutton's claim against Vivas. The claim that he returns us to imitation is related to the belief that his theory of archetypes implies that the poem is simply a representation or copy of a monomyth. If this is so, then Frye is open to the criticism that he is a sort of Platonist in the sense in which Ransom attacked Romantic theory as copying a "Platonic" realm.[20]

He anticipates this accusation; it is, after all, a traditional one. Whether he answers it adequately must be left to a more detailed analysis than we can embark on here. It is well to remember, however, that Frye insists on the *hypothetical* nature of his "literary universe," while Plato insisted on the reality of his realm of archetypes. The complaint that Frye condemns us to imitation as a form of copying is easy for some to make because of the inevitable disjunction between critical discourse with its mode of meaning and poetry with its mode of being. Just as the paraphrase cannot replace the poem, neither can critical discourse of the theoretical sort ever break through the paradoxes it must employ to describe how poetry acts. Thus criticism is, as we have learned in this examination of it, a language of repeated qualifications that often give to it, in the face of its object, a negative tone. Vivas must talk not only about creation and discovery but ultimately about creation *as* discovery. Frye must insist that imitation is not a matter of representation but of forming something. And so on back through Brooks on paradox, to Wilde, Sidney, Mazzoni, and the beginnings of critical theory. This is not an answer to the complaint or even an anticipation of how Frye would proceed to an answer, but an attempt to make out the grounds on which disagreement must be sharpened or resolved.

The second major objection to Frye is that he eschews judgments of value. Frye seems to consider criticism pre-evaluative. Good taste, which is the fundamental necessity of any value judgment worth entertaining, is developed by literary study. Literary study should be coherent and schematic enough to bring forth real knowledge of literary objects and to build up a concept of literature. Yet bad judgments will always be made by the most knowledgeable critics and good judgments by ig-

[20] John Crowe Ransom, "Poetry: A Note on Ontology" in *The World's Body* (New York: Scribner's, 1938).

norant ones. Frye believes value judgments are based upon direct experience, which is "central to criticism yet forever excluded from it. Criticism can account for it only in critical terminology, and that terminology can never recapture or include the original experience." [21] We are forced back upon the disjunction between the analytic nature of critical language and the untranslatable poem itself. For Frye criticism helps to build taste rather than to hand down judgments; in fact he argues: "Every deliberately constructed hierarchy of values in literature known to me is based on a concealed social, moral, or intellectual analogy." [22]

Beyond this we shall not go, except to indicate that in his discussion of these matters Frye provides insights that we can apply to the dilemma in which Richards leaves the reader in *Practical Criticism*. Richards points out and discusses the deficient responses of his students but never adequately explains why they make occasionally sophisticated responses. He can blame the failures on mnemonic irrelevances, sentimentalism, and so forth, but he does not examine why an occasional intelligent judgment is made. Frye allows for the possibility of good untutored taste, but he holds that taste is improved by knowledge. One can learn to read literature by learning the structural principles that criticism hypothesizes. The skill one develops should not be confused with the "subjective background of experience formed by his temperament and by every contact with words he has made." [23]

My own objection to Frye's argument is that he does not acknowledge what to me seems a philosophical assumption necessary to his position. I do not believe that he can hold to the philosophical neutrality of his method. Far into *Anatomy of Criticism* he insists that there are "extremely complicated philosophical problems" at every step of the argument, but obviously he wishes to avoid them and keep his method free and generally operable.[24] Perhaps he avoids a position so that the undeniably attractive aspects of his hypothesis sidestep fundamental philosophical resistance. However, refusal to take a position is itself a position or it masks a position not expressed or it is inconsistent. It strikes me that Frye does have a fundamental philosophical position and that it is neo-Kantian in the mode of Cassirer. In order for literature to be what he says it is, in order

[21] Frye, *Anatomy of Criticism*, p. 27.
[22] *Ibid.*, p. 23.
[23] *Ibid.*, p. 28.
[24] *Ibid.*, p. 350.

for the "literary universe" to be a workable hypothesis giving to literature all the cultural powers he wants it to have, I believe he must finally claim that there are no really centrifugal systems, that all systems are centripetal, that any system that claims centrifugality of meaning is simply insisting on a fiction that is one of its own structural laws. Furthermore, I believe that these systems must be considered in some sort of relation to each other, perhaps a relation of contrariety, of real opposition each to each other. We must find such resolution as logic can give us in paradox and strife.

If I am right, Frye belongs in the tradition we have been concerned with from Kant through the New Critics, even though there is a Hobbesian ring to his declarations and a Renaissance plenitude in his whole manner. He represents not a reversal of the dominant movement of early twentieth-century criticism, as some have held, but an attempt to extend it, joining it to anthropological criticism. But Frye tries to purge what is brought over from anthropology of its unliterary significances.

We have mentioned here the differences between the critical discourse and the language of the poem. Another critic, friendly to the New Criticism and deeply concerned with myth and anthropology, is Philip Wheelwright. In *The Burning Fountain,* Wheelwright lays the groundwork for his study of archetypes in literature and religion with an extended treatment of the difference between "steno language (the language of plain sense)" and "depth language (the language, broadly speaking of poetry)." [25] He combats the same positivism attacked by Allen Tate. The semantic positivist, according to Wheelwright, believes that "The only language that really means anything . . . is language which refers to things, events, and relations in the physical world. If it does not refer to the physical world, it does not refer to anything (for nothing else exists), and is therefore, strictly speaking, meaningless." [26]

He complains that the positivist relegates religious statements and literature to the meaningless even before the case has been heard. Wheelwright rejects the effort to reduce such statements to the rank of emotive utterance or to what Richards terms pseudo-statements. He moves toward distinguishing rather between the principles of expressive language and the assumptions of literal language. The former is depth language, the latter

[25] *The Burning Fountain* (Bloomington: Indiana Univ. Press, 1954), pp. 52–75.
[26] *Ibid.,* p. 31.

steno language. The symbols of literal language are semantically discrete, univocal, ideally invariable in meaning throughout a discourse, and either logically universal or existentially particular. For logical propositions Wheelwright formulates additional assumptions.

By contrast, expressive language, although it may exhibit the patterns mentioned above, can be iconic, plurisignative, soft of focus, contextual, expressive of other dimensions of meaning than the logical, variable in tone of assertion, and paradoxical. In Wheelwright's view literal language is the special form of language, depth language the general case.

He proceeds from these principles to a discussion of "confrontative imagining" with its "particularity of reference," "imaginative distancing," "archetypal imagining," and "metaphoric imagining." He finds these generally characteristic of poetic discourse. Poetry confronts the object, in the words of Martin Buber, as a "thou" rather than the lifeless "it" of logical discourse.[27] Poetry, however, does invite its own sort of distancing. Wheelwright uses the words of the aesthetician Edward Bullough to explain it. "It is putting the phenomenon, so to speak, out of gear with our practical, actual self." It is a "refusal to be concerned with the practical aspect of things." [28]

Wheelwright attempts to fuse the archetypal with particularity of confrontation, employing Goethe's distinction between symbolism and allegory and insisting that the universal is found in the poem in such a way that it cannot be divorced from the context and remain itself. He is attracted by Jung's idea that archetypes are preconsciously rooted symbols:

> I agree with Jung that the true philosopher is he who conceptualizes his ideas not at random, and not for the lone sake of consistency, but as transmutations of the "primitive and purely natural vision" which the archetypes express. When it comes to determining just what an archetype is, however, and how it operates and is transmitted, I fear that either Freud's or Jung's stubborn insistence upon the exclusive rights of a single method and a single theory tends to throw darkness on the path.[29]

Wheelwright is Kantian in his belief that knowledge takes place as a unifying act of the mind, but he desires to proceed beyond the merely conceptual unification of Kant to the idea of a "syn-

[27] See Martin Buber, *I and Thou,* 2nd ed. (New York: Scribner's 1958).
[28] Wheelwright, *op cit.,* p. 82.
[29] *Ibid.,* pp. 92–93.

thesis which expresses our actual living encounter with the world." [30] This synthesis would admit paradox, dramatic tension, and unresolved ambiguity. It would, we suppose, be achieved in the formulations of depth language.

Most of Wheelwright's book is a study of archetypes as they inhabit religion and literature. Perhaps this is the trouble. Although Wheelwright accepts the contextualist principle, in his attempt to reconstitute the idea of the universal in the literary work he seems sometimes, despite his protestations to the contrary, to give a sort of independent meaning and status to the archetype. The danger in this is reduction of the poem, after all, to a mere frame in which the archetype is displayed in all its preexisting universal significance. The depth language of the poem would not in this case be constitutive of the archetype's meaning at all. Instead, the poem would simply be appropriating the archetype's preordained power. Similarly, Wheelwright does not really provide us with the means of distinguishing a poem from a religious statement. All we seem to know is that archetypes abound in both and that both employ depth language.

As a result Frye seems more contextual than Wheelwright because of his insistence on the archetype as nothing more for the critic than a symbol that is repeated throughout literature as a structural principle, not a content or unit of meaning.

The approaches of critics interested in myth, ritual, and dream can, I think, be judged on the basis of whether in employing whatever insights they have they divest themselves of commitment to a reading of the work in terms of nonliterary concepts, using insights to clarify literary form rather than concepts to judge the content.

This has been the problem nearly endemic to critics interested in myth and ritual, anthropology and psychology. Creators of remarkable synthetic studies of archetypes, they have often been unable to establish workable differentia. Yet interesting and provocative work abounds in the field. The later writings of Gaston Bachelard (1884–1963), a philosopher of science, form a body of work throwing light upon problems of literary criticism. In studies of air, earth, fire, and water, Bachelard tried to build the basis for a "physics or chemistry of reverie." These ancient elements, no longer the elements of chemistry or nature, are in Bachelard's works the elements of imaginative experience. In *The Psychoanalysis of Fire* (1938) he concludes that his investigations of the imaginative element fire

[30] *Ibid.*, p. 69.

should offer new instruments for an objective literary criticism in the most precise sense of the term. It should demonstrate that metaphors are not simple idealizations which take off like rockets only to display their insignificance on bursting in the sky, but that on the contrary metaphors summon one another and are more coördinated than sensations, so much so that a poetic mind is purely and simply a syntax of metaphors.

The poet cannot be judged on Freudian, Jungian, Frazerian, or any other nonliterary grounds. Frye suggests that Freud's Oedipus complex may be an idea that exists now because something from which it could be drawn by allegorical commentary insisted in myth. To turn Freud's Oedipus complex back upon another literary work, interpreting it in the idea's light, is to go in a circle. A poem fully interpretable by allegorical commentary is not constitutive but imitative in the derogatory sense of the term. It has brought nothing to insistence. On the other hand, there may be in literature a structural principle that when conceptualized is apparently an analogue to the Oedipal situation. Frye, working out of Blake, and Bachelard in his book on fire both present such an analogue, and Frye remarks of it in his introduction to a recent translation of Bachelard's book. But this done, the particular poem still looms before us, and *in its light* the critic has yet to speak, though the business of criticism in respect to the "syntax of metaphor" may have been moved along very significantly.

The poet, incidentally, can make all sorts of preposterous psychological assertions in his poem and escape charges of defamation if the context properly assimilates them. As for the critic, his approach should be based on what he determines the context to be and upon his knowledge of what formal structures are likely in or characteristic of literature, not what school of anthropology or psychology particularly attracts his interest or assent. Otherwise the critic's reading asks us to judge the poem on the truth or falsity of its abstracted content or perhaps on the acceptability to the intellect of a whole nonliterary conceptual framework.

We have noted the appearance of imitation again in Frye's *Anatomy of Criticism.* This appearance coincides with the revival of Aristotelian language in the theoretical writings of several critics who were colleagues at the University of Chicago. Among these were Richard McKeon, R. S. Crane, Elder Olson, and Norman Maclean. In 1952, they published together a collection of essays entitled *Critics and Criticism,* which was followed by Crane's *The Languages of Criticism and the Structure of Poetry* (1953), the Alexander Lectures given at the University of Toronto in 1951–52. There is a similarity between Crane's idea of imitation and one of Frye's senses of the term, though on other matters there are disagreements between them.

The two books mentioned above are still the fundamental exhibits of a group now thought of as the new Aristotelians, neo-Aristotelians, or, for short, the Chicago critics. There have been later books, of course, but they do not fundamentally change the critical attitudes proposed in 1952 and 1953. This criticism revives wholesale the Aristotelian language and with it *mimesis*. Richard McKeon's "Literary Criticism and the Concept of Imitation in Antiquity," first published in 1935, and reprinted in *Critics and Criticism,* distinguishes between Plato's terminology and Aristotle's, showing that for Plato

> Not only arts, philosophy, and discourse are imitation. Human institutions must be added to the list. All governments are imitations of the true government; and the laws themselves, source of the true government, are imitations of particulars of the truth which are written down, so far as that is possible, from the dictation of those who know. But the expansion of the word "imitation" passes beyond human products, actions, virtues, and institutions; it extends to things themselves. All things change, imitating and following what happens to the entire universe; and the imitation conforms to its model even in conception, generation and nutrition. It extends finally to the first principles of things.[31]

In Aristotle there is no such development of a monolithic principle:

> Whereas for Plato the term "imitation" may undergo an infinite series of gradations of meaning, developed in a series of analogies, for Aristotle the term is restricted definitely to a single literal meaning . . . . whereas for Plato an exposition of the word "imitation" involves an excursion through all the reaches of his philosophy, "imitation" for Aristotle is relevant only to one restricted portion . . . .[32]

McKeon goes on to argue that for Aristotle the act of imitation is to separate "some form from the matter with which it is joined in nature," a form "perceptible by sensation," and then

[31] In R. S. Crane, ed., *Critics and Criticism* (Chicago: Univ. of Chicago Press, 1952), p. 153.
[32] *Ibid.,* p. 160.

join it to the "matter of his art," or the medium: "The action which he imitates may be 'natural' to the agent, but the artist must attempt to convey not that natural appropriateness and rightness, but rather a 'necessity or probability' suitably conveyed by the materials of his art." [33] McKeon allows for the likely impossibility approved by Aristotle; the likeliness is created by the particular formulation in the medium. Like Aristotle, he looks with less favor on the unlikely possibility, which would involve a wrenching of the shape of the whole in order to allow certain things to occur. McKeon proceeds to an illustration:

> The man who sits for his portrait assumes a posture which is determined by the laws of gravitation, by the anatomy of the human body, and by the peculiarities of his habits; the painter must justify the line he chooses not in terms of physics or anatomy, but in terms of the composition which appears in the colors and lines on his canvas. A man performs an action as a consequence of his character, his heritage, his fate, or his past actions; the poet represents that action as necessary in his medium, which is words, by developing the man's character, by expressing his thoughts and those of men about him, by narrating incidents. For Aristotle, consequently, imitation may be said to be, in the fine arts, the presentation of an aspect of things in a matter other than its natural matter, rendered inevitable by reasons other than its natural reasons.[34]

It is to be noted here that McKeon identifies imitation with representation, although he makes clear that in rendering an aspect of things in a foreign medium a new thing is created. Nevertheless, this raises the old epistemological questions all over again. What exactly is being copied? Are canons of accuracy to be applied? It would be difficult to do so, for the medium intervenes and is *supposed* to intervene, and seems finally more important than the representational element. If this is so, what is the point of the art object? The discussion of the portrait above leads us to conclude that some sort of criterion of accuracy indeed *must* be involved. Portraits are supposed to represent the people who have sat for them.

Or are they? Picasso is said to have remarked in answer to the criticism that Gertrude Stein did not resemble his portrait of her, "She will." Even when this Wildean view is adopted, *some* sort of relation is being insisted upon between object and

[33] *Ibid.*, p. 162.
[34] *Ibid.*

referent. McKeon does not seem to get around the old problem that imitation suggests some sort of criterion of accuracy, while our knowledge of the history of criticism tells us that introduction of the criterion tends to take us to a dead end.

It is true, however, that the more we think about McKeon's hypothetical portrait the less important its representational aspects become to our grasp of its reality, and the less important they are to McKeon himself. Judgment would finally have to be made on the basis of technique alone. But this tends to break the poem apart into technique and content and invites again a criterion of accuracy in the judgment of the content or simple dismissal of it. McKeon never quite gets the two together.

Perhaps this problem led Crane in *The Languages of Criticism and the Structure of Poetry* to venture forth with a new reading of Aristotle. The starting point is again imitation, but not quite the imitation of McKeon:

> An "imitation" is brought about whenever we succeed, by means of art, in producing an analogue of some natural process or form, endowed with similar powers to affect other things or us, in materials which are not necessarily disposed to assume of themselves any such process or form; any poem can thus be said to be an "imitation" when it is sufficiently intelligible, as a concrete whole, on the assumption that the poet, in making it, was intent on using certain possibilities of language in order to create in us, by certain devices of technique, the illusion of human beings more or less like ourselves doing or undergoing something, for the sake of the emotional effects naturally evoked by such characters, passions, or actions in real life when we view them as disinterested but sympathetic spectators.[35]

Two things are important here. First, the end of the poem is emotional effect, and cognitive power of any sort does not seem to be attributed to it. We shall return to this point later. Second, the idea of imitation seems to be different; the element of representation is ebbing out. This is clearer in a subsequent passage:

> Poems are not natural things, but the varieties of poems [Aristotle] proposes to speak of do have a kind of nature, that of being imitative structures made out of the mimetic possibilities of language. Their matter, as completed wholes, is a determinate selection and arrangement of words, and all the other elements are in a fundamental way contained in this medium and have no *poetic* being apart from what it permits. The object imitated is

[35] R. S. Crane, *The Languages of Criticism and the Structure of Poetry* (Toronto: Univ. of Toronto Press, 1953), p. 48.

internal and hence strictly "poetic" in the sense that it exists only as the intelligible and moving pattern of incidents, states of feeling, or images which the poet has constructed in the sequence of his words by analogy with some pattern of human experience such as men have either known or believed possible, or at least thought of as something that ought to be. This is not, then, a theory of poetry as "representation," with life set over against art as "a constant external reality" or subject-matter which art must somehow approximate or do justice to if it is to be good.[36]

Crane ends up by implying that the poem *creates* its own object of imitation, that the poem as words makes us infer a world of action, people, or whatever the poet hypothesizes as that to be imitated. Thus the object of the poem has no existence except as the internal creation of the poem through its medium, words. Gone is the simpler and, I think, more truly Aristotelian idea of McKeon.

Or is it gone after all? The outer world is suggested by the "analogy with some pattern of human experience such as men have known or believed possible or at least thought of as something that ought to be." But Crane denies that when he is speaking of the world he is speaking of the object imitated. It appears that he is trying valiantly to have it both ways, anchoring the poem in some sort of preconceived experiential pattern but insisting at the same time on the autonomy of the poem, saving imitation yet keeping it free of its usual meaning as representation of an external reality.

By describing the end of the poem as "emotional effects" and not insisting on cognitive power (of whatever kind) for poetry, Crane plays down the representational element in his theory but he cannot ever quite rationalize it away. It is finally made irrelevant to our interest in the poem; if the poet is not accurate in his representation, it makes no real difference since we are not going to judge it on its accuracy but on its existence as a poetic whole of a particular sort. Whether we are content to think of poetry's value only in terms of the emotion it conveys is a matter for some thought.

If Crane's Aristotle is the right one, then one wonders whether the term "imitation" is not finally an inadequate one, an unnecessary critical burden; for Crane, imitation no longer refers to what we commonly think of when the word appears; it concerns itself only with the relation of the poem to what the poem creates

[36] *Ibid.*, p. 56.

—its action, its plot, its character, as these things are pointed to by the words.

It is a fine point whether we should say that these things exist *in* the poem's language or are pointed to by the poem's words. A good amount of ink has been spilled over the distinction. Following Aristotle, the Chicago critics have found poetry to be composed of diction, plot, character, and so forth. They have been critical of those critics who have considered only the diction and in their eyes reduced poems to words alone. Elder Olson has attacked the method of William Empson in *Seven Types of Ambiguity*, accusing him of making a "tasteless muddle" of poetic texts because he has looked only at one dimension of poetic meaning. Olson's position is as follows:

> In the order of our coming to know the poem, it is true, the words are all-important; without them we could not know the poem. But when we grasp the structure we see that in the poetic order they are the least important element; they are governed by everything else in the poem. We are in fact far less moved by the words as mere words than we think; we think ourselves moved mainly by them because they are the only visible or audible part of the poem. As soon as we grasp the grammatical meaning of an expression in a mimetic poem, we begin drawing inferences which we scarcely recognize as inferences, because they are just such as we habitually make in life; inferences from the speech as to the character, his situation, his thought, his passion, suddenly set the speaker vividly before us and arouse our emotions in sympathy or antipathy.[37]

There is no doubt about Empson's excesses in his book, and Olson is understandably harsh with him. But whether Olson is theoretically impeccable himself is another matter. He complains that the New Critics generally reduce all poems to words and therefore overlook matters of plot and character. But Olson's argument, although it makes a telling criticism of New Critical practice, may not really touch its theory. The New Critical interest cannot be described properly as an interest in the poem's words. The interest is in the poem as a language. Rather than emphasizing what the words of the poem point to, the New Critics tended to emphasize what the poem makes *in* language. It is finally a matter of epistemology, the New Criticism implying that language is constitutive of reality in a symbolic form, while Olson seems to hold that words are fundamentally denotative,

[37] Elder Olson, "William Empson, Contemporary Criticism, and Poetic Diction" in Crane, ed., *Critics and Criticism*, p. 55.

pointing to things. The question is the degree of actual being we can attribute to what in Olson's terms the poem points to. It can hardly be real in any sense, for it is cut off from the real world by the filtering medium: "Just as tragedy is not a thing existing by nature, what is imitated is different from the imitation of it: plot is not action but action imitated, and character and thought are not what they are in life, but what they are as imitated in a poem." [38] Thus, on the one hand, the poem seems to be isolated from a denotative or representational relation to experience, and, on the other, the poem as a linguistic structure is not considered as constitutive of reality, that is, as organizing experience in constitutive symbols. The poem, then, as in Crane, seems to be justified only in terms of its emotive effect.

Crane, himself, is driven to a kind of Crocean position as he apparently tries to escape from this dilemma. He nearly cuts the poem off from direct reference to anything external to it. In his last chapter he claims that the writer has a sort of intuition of what he will make: "more than a general intention, more than a 'theme,' and more than an outline in the usual sense of that word; it is, as I have said, a shaping or directing cause . . . ." [39] But then, like Croce, he remarks (knowing that his idea of intuition leads him back to the idea of the poem as a representation of the intuition): "He can know what he can do, in fact, only after he has done it; and the doing is an act of synthesis which, if it is successful, inevitably imposes a new character on the materials and devices out of which it is effected." [40]

Crane has argued mightily in his book against the inadequacies of many positions only to return, it seems to me, to one that threatens to collapse of its own terminology. Perhaps his real enemy is discursive language itself, the enemy of all critics, a medium inadequate to the job, never quite fine enough an instrument to make the discriminations it forces on itself. Finally, he almost embraces the idea of language as constitutive, for if the poet knows what he has done only when he has got it into the medium, this indicates that the language has really *created* the intuition. Crane here seems driven toward Vivas, who attacks the whole doctrine of imitation as well as the idea of expression and concludes that the function of art for which there is no

[38] Elder Olson, *Aristotle's "Poetics" and English Literature* (Chicago: Univ. of Chicago Press, 1965), p. xviii.
[39] Crane, *The Languages of Criticism and the Structure of Poetry,* p. 141.
[40] *Ibid.,* p. 144.

substitute is "to organize the primary data of experience by means of the creation of constitutive symbols." [41]

From the foregoing discussions it appears that there is an ineradicable Romantic irony in the enterprise of criticism. Like the quest of the Byronic hero, it is endless and yet at the same time valuable—endless because its terms are finally self-defeating, and valuable because in its own inadequacy it calls attention to the greater adequacy of the poem itself, which manages to say or be more than remarks about it can ever say. For this reason, it is possible to characterize criticism as fundamentally negative. It is always denying the adequacy of *any* critical statement and constantly urging us to look again. At the same time it does not negate the value of those statements of which it denies the adequacy. It accepts the ironic relation between art and discussions of art. Although endless, criticism can perform an important function, both revealing the work of art and warning against the terms of the revelation.

This is not to suggest that our problem is that works of art change their meaning (or being) as time passes and therefore their meaning is reinterpretable in every age. Their meaning remains the same and in most cases must be recovered. Our own language changes, and thus the terms of our critical discourse change. Criticism must thus renew itself. To say that the meaning of literary works remains the same is, of course, not to say that meaning is fully discoverable or subject to conceptualization.

Recent critical speculation is enamored of the paradoxical situation of criticism itself, honing the distinction between criticism and literature to a fine edge. The critical speculation influenced by phenomenology and existentialism is particularly related to this situation. Both were born of the effort to obliterate the subject-object gulf. In Edmund Husserl's doctrine of "intentionality" there is the effort to re-establish the reality of appearances, not by insisting that appearances are reality because they are in the mind of the perceiver and everything is mind (as in Berkeley) but by insisting that objects are indeed their appearances and that all else is a fiction. In a discussion of Husserl, E. W. Knight writes:

> For the first time, with such application, philosophers are proposing that everything be considered as known. The world is exactly

[41] Eliseo Vivas, "Animadversions on Imitation and Expression" in *The Artistic Transaction* (Columbus: Ohio State Univ. Press, 1963), p. 168.

what it appears to us to be. Appearance instead of being an un-
reliable subjective flux, is truth itself; or, as Husserl says, "It
would be absurd to deny value to 'I see it' when the question
at issue is 'Why?'" It is difficult for us not to think of Reality,
Being, Truth, or whatever term we prefer, as the product of
painstaking investigation, if we consider it inaccessible at all—
in actual fact it is the very stuff of life. "The world is not what
I think, but what I live." In what concerns our knowledge of
matter, reason leads us astray. For example, there is no intellec-
tion involved in my perception of a brown house; there is no
joining together of two "things" in the mind, brown and house,
to produce brown house. I can, if I wish, make the colour brown
of the house the object of a particular perception, but ordinarily
what I perceive is a brown house, and not a colour to be added
subjectively to the perception of a house. Primary and secondary
qualities are derived notions, they have no place in everyday
perception, because objects *are* their appearances and not an
aggregate of qualities assembled in the mind.[42]

Phenomenology has tried to "put back together again what
philosophy has analysed into incomprehensibility." [43] The results of this for critical theory are at least twofold: Emphasis is
thrown upon the necessity of particular as against abstract
knowledge, and if literature is a means of getting at the particular
by way of language, then literature would suddenly seem to be
the true form of philosophy itself. The language of logical statement is naturally analytical and divisive, while the poem
attempts to intend the object by verbal means.

Some phenomenological discussions of literature have tended
to praise poems that seem to make assertions like those of Knight
above. William Carlos Williams' famous poem about the red
wheelbarrow is looked upon with great favor:

> so much depends
> upon
>
> a red wheel
> barrow
>
> glazed with rain
> water
>
> beside the white
> chickens

---

[42] E. W. Knight, *Literature Considered as Philosophy* (New York: Collier,
1962), pp. 38–39.
[43] *Ibid.*, p. 40.

However, if so much depends upon the red wheelbarrow, then it seems that poems that are statements to this effect unnecessarily *stand between* the reader and the object itself. Better indeed would be an "intention" of the wheelbarrow than of the poem. The value of the poem would only be the act that it points us toward; its language would be viewed only as referential, and the split between content and technique would again be affirmed. It would be possible to write a book about poetry with little or no attention to technique. All of the problems of imitation are again raised and the status of the poem as an object itself is tacitly called in question. The desire to treat the poem as the ultimate mode of philosophy is the result of wanting to return to particularity, just as Blake argued for particularity in his criticism of Reynolds; but one wonders whether this is not self-defeating if in the process literature is in turn to be reduced to its philosophical *content* by those praising it.

What phenomenology perhaps finally does properly affirm is that, like the brown house, which is held together by phenomenology but broken into parts by modes of analysis, the poem must be held together too by the critic's intention of it and not divided into form and content. There is *one* poem to be intended in all its variety *and* its totality. There are no discrete approaches to the poem, only the critic's intention of it or his failure to understand it. And there is no mode of analysis that isolates an aspect of the poem. An aspect is not the poem or even a part of the poem any longer.[44] But as long as one sees the poem as a representation of a brown house in nature, the poem is reduced to a representation of the intention, and we fall back into all those familiar problems surrounding imitation that have led modern critics to attribute a constitutive power to poems.

The phenomenologist cannot quite allow the poem this constitutive power, for he wishes to attribute knowable existence to things in themselves without the mediation of language. Perhaps it is better to say that the poem represents not the intention of the brown house but the poetic act of intending it. This would return us to problems we have already discussed with respect to Schelling and the Romantics. The poem would be a copy of the act, unless we take the view that the intention is not previous to the poem and does not exist except in its poetic formulation. This in turn makes the particular world of the phenomenologist dissolve into the verbal system that constitutes it. We are re-

[44] See the introduction to Geoffrey H. Hartman, *The Unmediated Vision* (New Haven, Conn.: Yale Univ. Press, 1954).

turned to Crocean intuition or to Cassirer's form of neo-Kantianism. We know only what our language makes.

This is surely an interesting dilemma. It could be stated in a variety of other ways. I am inclined to think that it is a dilemma caused by the bewitchment of language. But I believe that the bewitchment is ironically inevitable no matter which way we turn. We must develop our critical strategies with this ironical understanding of the limits of our verbal instruments well in mind.

But with sufficient irony and constant concern for an analysis of the play of the medium in any literary theory, the critic can often discover in the creative thought of those engaged in the disciplines around him suggestions that he may pursue in his own speculation, though they will have to be transmuted ultimately into structural principles of the poem rather than bold assertions that this or that is so. Surely the great critics have always been open to suggestions from all of their experience. Aristotle and Coleridge, to name only two of the greatest, had far-ranging intellects and did not seem content until they were able to place their theory of literature in its relation to their other theories. In the contemporary critic Kenneth Burke we see a similar curiosity and search for synthesis that takes him into psychology, politics, anthropology, and other areas. Cassirer moved from a critique of science to a critique of culture, which included a study of art. Frye's *The Modern Century* (1967) has demonstrated how a social criticism can be evolved from a literary theory.

It has been clear at least since Frazer and Harrison that philosophical anthropology, with its interest in language and myth, sometimes nearly turns into literary criticism. Most anthropologists now believe Frazer erred in interpreting the meaning of his data, but once the literary critic considers Frazer's structures of myth and ritual, he may begin to think about literature as if it had structures, too. It may or may not have structures analogous to anything else, and if it does, this may or may not prove anything. In any case, the suggestion of synthesis is there and it may be most fruitful.

We see this in the relation that has developed between structural linguistics and anthropology. Ferdinand de Saussure's posthumous *Cours de linguistique générale* (1915) provided Claude Levi-Strauss with a method of analysis that he transferred into the field of anthropology, particularly in his studies of kinship and totemism and in his later book, *The Savage Mind*

(1962). A link to literary criticism is present in the long and prolific career of Roman Jakobson. Jakobson was the leader of the Russian school of formalist criticism that flourished early in this century and independently developed many of the principles of the New Criticism.[45] Jakobson made considerable contributions to linguistic theory as well as to literary criticism and has recently collaborated with Levi-Strauss on a structural analysis of Baudelaire's *Les Chats*.[46] The question of structuralism is whether the idea of linguistic structure, which Levi-Strauss claims is applicable to societies, is also applicable to literature. In some respects, and perhaps fundamentally, this principle of structure comes historically from a formalist literary theory and is turned back upon it in a monolithic way. The formalist held that every poem was in itself a system. As de Saussure had argued for the systematic structure of a language, Levi-Strauss argued in *The Savage Mind* for the systematic nature of savage logic, namely classification, which is always present but organized on its own terms. The principle of structure is that if one is given several sets, one may not compare the separate data from one set to those of another. Instead, only the total systems may be compared. The principle is a contextualist one.

But structuralism applied to literature departs from, say, Russian formalism when it goes beyond the analysis of single works and thinks of literature itself as a sort of monolithic object with structures. Thus, in the description of structuralism offered by a recent commentator we find: "a new kind of criticism which could view literature as an institution with its own laws or structural principles, yet relate these to both local traditions and the societal as such." [47] This cuts a broad swath and includes among structuralists Frye and perhaps Cassirer, much as they might disagree with Levi-Strauss on a number of matters. We begin to suspect that formalist literary theory may have been the seed of linguistic and anthropological structuralism rather

---

[45] See Victor Erlich, *Russian Formalism: History, Doctrine*, 2nd rev. ed. (The Hague: Mouton, 1965). Also Ewa Majewska Thompson, "Russian Formalism and Anglo-American New Criticism: A Comparative Study," unpublished doctoral dissertation, Vanderbilt University, 1967.

[46] Roman Jakobson and Claude Levi-Strauss, "Les Chats de Baudelaire," *L'Homme*, Vol. 2, No. 1 (1962), pp. 5–21. But see the criticism of their method by Michael Riffaterre, "Describing Poetic Structures: Two Approaches to Baudelaire's *les Chats*," *Yale French Studies*, Vols. 36–37 (1966), pp. 200–42.

[47] Geoffrey Hartman, "Structuralism: The Anglo-American Adventure," *Yale French Studies*, Vols. 36–37 (1966), p. 151.

than the other way around. Surely the career of Jakobson suggests this; surely the literary theorist not only receives inspiration from other disciplines but is capable of dispensing it as well.

It is difficult, however, to square the Russian formalists' almost total concern with the medium with Levi-Strauss's emphasis as an anthropologist on a sort of naive imitation at one time and with his characterization of the artist as "always mid-way between design and anecdote" at another. He also speaks of an "aesthetic emotion," thus swinging between a criticism emphasizing the artist and one emphasizing the observer.[48] It is doubtful that there is anything particularly new in his remarks about art, and to the literary theorist there is not enough rigor in his discourse. Structuralism has seemed to move from the concern with language expressed by its relation to linguistics toward analysis of structures in the depths of the mind that leads to poems, myths, dreams, and so forth, thus threatening to abandon the medium.

But this returns us to the reason for discussing structuralism in the first place. When Levi-Strauss studies primitive logic or when he attempts to establish systematic relationships between linguistic structure and primitive social structures, he is, like Bachelard, exploring the possibility of analogies. His work may prove useful to the literary theorist in ways we do not yet understand.

[48] Claude Levi-Strauss, *The Savage Mind* (Chicago: Univ. of Chicago Press, 1966), pp. 24–27.

# 7 SYSTEM AND VIOLENCE

Ezra Pound once observed, "There is nothing easier than to be distracted from one's point, or from the main drive of one's subject by a desire for utterly flawless equity and omniscience." This remark provides an opportunity for turning from a discussion of systematic literary theory toward what I shall call "violent criticism." Perhaps it is better to say that I am turning to violent *critics*. Actually one seldom finds pure violence or pure system, purely violent critics or purely systematic ones. Instead, one finds tendencies. Critics tending toward violence are likely to parade themselves each as his own man. Violent criticism therefore takes a Protean character. Critics who characteristically practice it often refuse to develop a theoretical position in much detail. At the extreme of violence they aim directly at evaluation of specific discrete literary works rather than inquiry into such things as the nature of a poem or of literature in general. Violent critics are often polemical in the extreme and polemical for or against a certain poetic fashion or school. As a group, violent critics provide the contrary of the systematic critics with whom we have been concerned.

By "contrary" I mean what William Blake had in mind when he wrote: "Without contraries is no progression." [1] He was distinguishing between a "contrary" and a "negation," holding that life proceeds by prolific opposition, not by wholesale obliteration of the opposite. We have seen that the systematic critic attempts the Olympian view of literature as a whole, or literature as a community of different kinds of objects, or literature as a way of

[1] In *The Marriage of Heaven and Hell.*

knowing, or literature as a way of teaching or entertaining or expressing the self. In the case of these critics the effort is to reach definitions and make distinctions. All of this is important, for it leads us to a greater insight into what we are about, what the poet does, what he does not do, and what literature has to do with culture. But literature itself and literary theory have also thrived on and probably depended on a kind of talk about literature that from the vantage of pure system seems irresponsible. System must grudgingly accept it because it is creative of insights in spite of its disdain of method.

Unending struggle, complete with vituperation, passes between systematic and violent critics. Violent critics like to think of system-makers as unimaginative soulless creatures who have no real appreciation of art and devour it for the sake of the system they construct. The attacks of violent critics, who often have the advantage over their contraries in poetic skill, range all the way from *ad hominem* prose ridicule to such bardic spells as:

> Lo the Bat with Leathern wing,
> Winking & blinking
> Winking & blinking
> Winking & blinking
> Like Doctor Johnson.[2]

Today violent critics tend to associate system with the academy; they talk with condescension of academic poetry and academic critics. Northrop Frye remarks that such gestures are part of the literary convention requiring that poets bite the hands that feed them. He is probably right, since at the present time most such attacks come from critics and poets on university payrolls.[3]

The systematic critic is usually an academician but often as haughty and disdainful of his English department colleagues as the violent critic is of him. He has had his own fights with traditional literary scholarship. He finds some violent criticism helpful, and he often assimilates its insights to the bloodstream of his own ideas. Violent criticism is often engendered by poets interested in propagating their own species of poem. Since in the previous chapters we have noticed a definite irony in the situation of the system-maker, it is well to recognize an irony in the

---

[2] From Blake's "An Island in the Moon."
[3] *Approaches to the Study of Twentieth-Century Literature,* Proceedings of the Conference in the Study of Twentieth-Century Literature, 1st Session (East Lansing: Michigan State Univ., 1961), pp. 164–65.

situation of the violent critic as well. If he succeeds in propagating his species, then it too is amenable to systematizing and it is likely that he will become disenchanted with the results and either divorce himself from the movement or complain about its corruption in the hands of lesser artists. (Thus Ezra Pound came to attack Imagism as Amygism after Amy Lowell appropriated it.)

Despite all the curiosities of violent criticism and all its spilled ink and often silly invective, it is important. Even its vulgar horn-tooting is often noisy in behalf of important literary causes. Without the noise one wonders whether some great poems would ever have received a hearing. Often, too, the most sensitive reading and elucidation comes from the arena of literary violence.

I propose to look briefly at a few examples of violent criticism even though the aim of the book has been to examine problems discovered by system. In this age one thinks first, I suppose, of Ezra Pound. The most pristine sort of violent critic must have impeccable antiacademic credentials. This is important so that no other violent critics can mount the *ad hominem* antiprofessional attack upon him, causing him to lose some of his potential audience in advance of being heard. Pound does have the flaw of possessing academic degrees, but he is redeemed by having been dismissed from a teaching job at Wabash College shortly into his first year. G. S. Fraser's account is tonally correct, though I shall not vouch for the facts: "He showed, I have been told, an innocent protective interest in a chorus girl or ballet dancer stranded in Crawfordsville down on her luck . . . ." [4] Fraser attributes Pound's antiacademism to his dismissal. I prefer to consider the event a symptom, not the cause. Pound deserves the right to a free abstract distaste.

In any case, a convention of violent criticism is well illustrated by the first few paragraphs of Pound's "How to Read," where professors of literature are attacked. According to Pound, those professors who approach their subject with a drill manual rise to greatest success in the profession, while those who really have some aptitude for understanding poetry remain "obscurely in less exalted positions." [5] Presumably the best are fired. A violent critic more inventive than Pound on this point might have worked out the convention's possibilities by insisting that the

[4] G. S. Fraser, *Ezra Pound* (New York: Grove Press, 1961), p. 10.
[5] Ezra Pound, "How to Read" in *Literary Essays of Ezra Pound,* ed. by T. S. Eliot (London: Faber & Faber, 1954), p. 16.

very best never get hired at all and that the geniuses never even make themselves available.

Pound's violence is of two sorts. First, there are his polemics in behalf of certain kinds of poetry. Second, there are his evaluations of poets of the past. His propaganda in behalf first of Imagism and then of Vorticism may not have a permanent value in itself, but it has had an inestimable influence. His "A Retrospect" does not tell us how all poems ought to be written, but anyone can sense in reading the essay that it is a clear attack on excesses a poet should avoid: "To begin with, consider the three propositions (demanding direct treatment, economy of words, and the sequence of the musical phrase), not as dogma —never consider anything as dogma—but as the result of long contemplation, which even if it is someone else's contemplation, may be worth consideration." [6] Pound proceeds to lay down a whole series of "don'ts": Don't use superfluous words, avoid mixtures of abstractions and concretions like "dim lands of peace," generally fear abstractions, and so forth. Fundamentally what he is doing is expressing the negative side of the Imagist manifesto. But he abandoned the Imagist movement when it seemed to him to have failed in practice.

Pound developed a simple, flexible, pragmatic terminology sufficient to express what he wanted to say about poetry. Its key words are three terms from the Greek: *melopoeia, phanopoeia,* and *logopoeia. Melopoeia* is the musical or oral character of verse, *phanopoeia* "the casting of images upon visual imagination," *logopoeia* "the dance of intellect among words." [7] As a critic Pound has seemed to be most interested in *melopoeia,* although the *phanopoeia* of the Chinese written character as well as Imagism has attracted his attention from time to time. In both "How to Read" and the later *ABC of Reading,* Pound makes lists of poets who were true inventors, and these lists seem devised mainly, but not wholly, upon the bases of invention in *melopoeia.*[8] He has consistently found such inventions in places not familiar to the current literary historians. The value of Pound's criticism lies more in its effect upon poetic practice than upon critical practice. But poetic practice, of course, eventually affects critical practice, requiring new emphases. Pound helped create American interest in oriental poetry and Provençal verse, even though his translations of such poems are hardly translations

[6] *Ibid.,* p. 4.
[7] *Ibid.,* p. 25.
[8] Ezra Pound, *ABC of Reading* (New York: New Directions, 1960), p. 79.

in the usual sense and have been thought laughable by many erudite scholars. Perhaps no single critic has had more influence on twentieth-century American poetic practice than Pound presenting his "exhibits" of inventiveness in *ABC of Reading*, reviving interest in Provençal poetry in *The Spirit of Romance*, or discussing art in the remarkable book *Gaudier-Brzeska*.

Over a period of years until his incarceration in St. Elizabeth's Hospital after World War II, Pound issued a series of statements about what a poet does and what poetry should be. These remarks often boil down to a demand for accuracy and sincerity, which in turn mean fidelity to the artistic function. The artist gives us "our best data for determining what sort of creature man is": "The serious artist is scientific in that he presents the image of his desire, of his hate, of his indifference as precisely that, as precisely the image of his own desire, hate or indifference. The more precise his record the more lasting and unassailable his work of art." [9] This is a simple statement on the surface and is meant to be taken as such. We can subject it to extended thought in the light of the preceding chapters of this book. We may quickly decide that it is not very original, that it is even simple-minded. Clearly, there is a lot of vagueness in it. Terms like "scientific" and "precise" are vaguely used. We could point out the Romantic expressive tendencies in it and worry the precise meaning of "image." But we would be, I think, taking it in a way in which it was not offered. Pound is not a systematic thinker. He is better with the detached insight, and his whole style indicates that he is aware of this. *ABC of Reading* is not a book that moves in a straight line but a collection of verbal blasts. They have the effect of building up a total attitude, a single spirit. In *ABC of Reading* he remarks: "To put it another way, I am, after all these years, making a list of works that I still re-read; that I keep on my desk and look into now and again." [10] Pound's criticism is an attempt to get us to those books for what to him is their obvious value.

The aphoristic, the blasting, or the nonlinear style is typical of many poets when they come to write criticism or any prose. (The case is often even more extreme with painters and sculptors.) This is probably because their thought processes are trained to the demands of their own medium. Their prose pieces are likely to evolve their own unique structures. We find this to be true in such diverse works as Ben Jonson's

[9] "The Serious Artist" in Eliot, *op cit.*, p. 46.
[10] Pound, *ABC of Reading*, p. 49.

*Discoveries,* William Butler Yeats's work of the same name, and W. H. Auden's "Squares and Oblongs" as well as his larger book *The Enchafed Flood.* It is clear that this has something to do with the difficulty of Wallace Stevens' *The Necessary Angel* when the book is approached as if it were a piece of clearly expository prose. The prefaces of Henry James are not immune to the same description. Blake's best criticism is spread mainly through marginalia but never systematically set down.

An aspect of violent criticism not to be underestimated is the way in which it often helps to elucidate the poetic aims and even the poems of its author, even when the author may not be writing about his own work. No matter what else they do, the essays of T. S. Eliot provide all sorts of insights into Eliot's poetry. Eliot's treatment of Milton, for example, reveals his own preoccupations. Pound's essays are nearly indispensable as criticism of his own poems. Edith Sitwell's essays on prosody, as much as we admire her rough and ready ability to discuss the rhythmic and sound patterns of others, remain fundamental to an understanding of her own experiments. At the same time we would be foolish to take seriously her opinions on many things. Her insistence that Swinburne was a Christian, for example, tells us more about her poetry than about Swinburne's.[11]

In these matters the violent critic who is a poet has a great advantage over the workmanlike but unoriginal systematic critic, who would guard himself sedulously against making Sitwellian exuberances. The poet's worst criticism elucidates his work and therefore develops a special importance. An excellent example is probably the Clark Lectures of 1954–55 given by Robert Graves at Trinity College, Cambridge, and published in *The Crowning Privilege.* Grave's tour through English poetry is eccentric and cranky. The last lecture, "These Be Your Gods, O Israel!," is perhaps the most remarkable example of articulated professional jealousy of our age. Graves attacks in order Yeats, Pound, Eliot, and Dylan Thomas, his ostensible point being that the public has too quickly erected monuments to these poets (some not yet dead). A secondary aim no doubt is to call attention to those not canonized, including Graves. Unfortunately Graves's attacks are usually irrelevant, inaccurate, and *ad hominem.* Even so there is a point:

> the ancients at least waited until Homer and Virgil were decently
> dead before they paid them heroic honours. The living poet

[11] Edith Sitwell, *Swinburne: A Selection* (New York: Harcourt, Brace & World, 1960), p. 47.

hero is a modernism; I think I am right in saying that Petrarch was the first poet to receive quasi-divine honours during his lifetime. And once an idol is set up it cannot easily be removed . . . .[12]

Graves's lectures with their occasional remarks about prosody and his somewhat fictional view of the professional life of the earliest English poets, tell us quite a bit about Graves's poetry and its central concerns. Of course, his "grammar of poetic myth," *The White Goddess,* tells us even more, exhibiting a curious scholarship to try to prove that all true poetry from the time of the ancient Celts is "religious invocation of the Muse." [13]

The performance of *The White Goddess* is similar in some ways to Yeats's *A Vision,* which can also be viewed as an attempt at a grammar of literary symbolism, though very obliquely presented. Again, in *A Vision,* all question of the book's artistic merit aside, the poet helps to elucidate his own method and perhaps the method of other poets. Yeats does not do this in any literal way but rather suggests what the interests of the poet are and to some extent organizes them for us. It is possible that we may expect more such books in an age of poets self-conscious about the tradition in which they work and in an age of contextualism, where exterior interpretive principles are less trusted than an inquiry into the shaping structure of each work. Wallace Stevens' posthumous "Adagia" performs a similar function, and one notices that Theodore Roethke's posthumous collection of essays turns back consistently to his own poems or to himself as a poet.[14]

We tend to think of dead poet-critics as less violent than they seemed to their contemporaries. William Wordsworth comes on now with a grandfatherly beard, but his preface to the second edition of *Lyrical Ballads* is definitely violent criticism and admittedly an attempt to create the taste by which he would be appreciated. Systematizers came later to organize a whole theory on the expressive principles Wordsworth tossed off in his preface. The same is probably true of the erudite Philip Sidney, who clearly had read or knew of the Italian systematic interpreters of Aristotle but was using his knowledge of their principles to counterattack derogators of the poetic art. We think highly of

[12] Robert Graves, *The Crowning Privilege* (Garden City, N.Y.: Doubleday, 1956), p. 120.
[13] Robert Graves, *The White Goddess* (New York: Creative Age, 1948), *passim.*
[14] Theodore Roethke, *On the Poet and His Craft* (Seattle: Univ. of Washington Press, 1965).

these critics, whether we judge them violent or not. Unfortunately violence is not a sure sign of critical genius. It is well to remember that Thomas Rymer thought *Othello* a "bloody farce."

Violent critics need not be poets, at least not great or famous poets. Perhaps the best-known violent academician is F. R. Leavis of Cambridge, whose criticism has perhaps had a greater effect on the teaching of literature in England than that of anyone since Matthew Arnold. In America, only Cleanth Brooks and Robert Penn Warren have had a comparable effect. In some minds Leavis has been linked with the New Critics of America, but in fact his methods have not generally been those of close textual analysis such as we find in the work of Brooks. In taste, however, there is some similarity between his *Revaluation* (1936) and Brooks's *Modern Poetry and the Tradition* (1939). They have in common the influence of T. S. Eliot. Brooks raises up the metaphysicals and the moderns at the expense of the Romantic poets. Leavis makes a similar judgment against the Romantics, and the metaphysicals are glorified. Leavis' discipleship of Eliot is clear. His first book, *New Bearings in English Poetry* (1932), presented cases for Eliot, Pound, and Gerard Manley Hopkins, generally in terms of Eliot's own statements. In an epilogue written for the 1950 edition, Leavis describes the state of criticism in England at the time he wrote the book as downright hostile to Eliot; he believes that his book may have done much to change the prevailing taste.

The later Leavis had to put up with an Eliot who occasionally changed his views or who in later years did not adopt critical attitudes Leavis thought he should have. That this has been an annoyance to Leavis is particularly apparent in the last chapter of Leavis' book *D. H. Lawrence: Novelist* (1955), in which he takes his former leader to task for a sort of grudging belated condescension to Lawrence's achievement. The book on Lawrence is Leavis at perhaps his most violent. There is little of the useful violence of *New Bearings* here, only the shouting of someone who seems to know no other tune. It goes hand in hand with a certain garrulousness in the commentary on Lawrence's novels themselves. The pattern of Leavis' criticism was clearly established by the first book. He was to be the champion of insufficiently respected writers. He would relocate the tradition in the face of a conspiratorial literary establishment. *The Great Tradition* (1948) attempts for fiction what *New Bearings* tried to do for poetry. In the meantime, however, T. S. Eliot had *become* the establishment, and he had therefore to be cut down to size for the sake of the unaristocratic outsider Lawrence. Leavis has consistently made comparative judgments between writers without clearly enunciating any general principles of art. This has occasionally made him and his own disciples (and they are legion by now) appear silly or vindictive. Yet he has performed a real service as a gadfly in the realm of literary politics.

The American critic most like him, but with a much more clearly explained theoretical base, is Yvor Winters (1900–67). Winters was a champion of various "neglected" writers, a fearless debater, and at times a very sensitive reader of poems. He attacked the critical language of John Crowe Ransom and the poetry of Ransom's students.[15] Yet he acknowledged the strengths that he found in some of Ransom's poems. He worked hard to establish the critical reputation of poets barely known to most American readers: Jones Very, Frederick Goddard Tuckerman, Adelaide Crapsey. He was outspoken about the establishment: "Emerson had talent, which was badly damaged by foolish thinking; Bryant might be described as a fine second-rate poet, better than most of the British poets of the century. Of Poe and Whitman, the less said the better." [16] Even with Tuckerman he was ready to call a bad line a bad line. Writing of one of Tuckerman's best sonnets, he observed:

> The first four lines are excellent, the next three respectable; the eighth again is excellent. The ninth is as good as the first four; the tenth is a sentimental stereotype. In the last five lines, we have one of the most beautiful descriptions in nineteenth-century poetry, but marred again by the second of these lines.[17]

This is the critic as evaluator with a magnifying glass; it is also part of an honest effort to find out strengths and weaknesses and why they are as they are.

Winters was an admirer of Emily Dickinson, but he did not fail to excoriate a poem that seemed weak to him, the poem about a locomotive: "The poem is abominable; and the quality of silly playfulness which renders it abominable is diffused more or less perceptibly throughout most of her work, and this diffusion is facilitated by the limited range of her metrical

[15] "John Crowe Ransom, or Thunder Without God" in *In Defense of Reason* (Denver: Swallow, 1951), pp. 502–55.
[16] Yvor Winters' Foreword to N. Scott Momaday, ed., *The Complete Poems of Frederick Goddard Tuckerman* (New York: Oxford Univ. Press, 1965), p. ix.
[17] *Ibid.*, p. x.

schemes." [18] Winters' admiration is fundamentally for poems, less for poets. In his view, very few poems or, for that matter, critical statements pass the test of close scrutiny.

To have included Winters among the violent critics, when he argued theoretically with Ransom and others, is probably to invite the charge of inconsistency. My reason for including him is that when he is confronting lines and stanzas he is at his best. In an age of criticism that has prized itself on the close reading and evaluation of texts it is surprising how little confrontation of this sort has actually occurred and how little evaluation has come with it when it has. This is one reason that Winters, who always speaks his mind, seems violent. There are other reasons too, however, as a reading of his violent criticism of Yeats will show: It is irresponsible, not closely enough argued; only occasionally does witty invective pull Winters through. Finally, Winters was a teacher, who must be always a little violent to keep his class, the reader, awake, to make him read carefully and with discrimination.

Winters' *In Defense of Reason* contains a part entitled "A Brief Selection of the Poems of Jones Very," and in his essay on Emily Dickinson several poems are printed in full as exhibits of Dickinson at her best.[19] These in a sense are brief anthologies designed to change and improve taste. Ezra Pound's "exhibits" in *ABC of Reading* form an anthology of innovations. Anthologies are violent criticism of the most formidable sort. America's taste for its own poets has been strongly affected by the activities of its anthologists. An interesting book could be written on the major anthologies of American poetry. It would begin with E. C. Stedman's collections in the nineteenth century and work up through Louis Untermeyer and Oscar Williams to Donald Allen's *New American Poetry* and Hall, Pack, and Simpson's *The New Poets of England and America*. If we were to enlarge our interest to include American anthologies of English verse, we would need to note Brooks and Warren's *Understanding Poetry* and the many college texts since published. The latter would be less interesting, since most such collections are made out of response to some vague sense of public taste. They do not try to form or reform that taste. Of course, it is not always easy to uncover the premises of taste on which an anthology has been made. Pound's and Winters' are clear enough. So are Brooks and Warren's.

---

[18] Yvor Winters, "Emily Dickinson and the Limits of Judgment" in *In Defense of Reason*, p. 284.
[19] *Ibid.*, pp. 344–57, pp. 283–99.

Violent criticism meets and quarrels with system precisely where taste and theory rub against one another. More often than not this rubbing is abrasive. Much has been said about the gulf between interpretation and evaluation; much has been written condemning the existence of the gulf. It is a crucial concern, and it is taken up here by way of conclusion with no answers promised. Generally we discover that systematic literary theorists tend to develop theories of interpretation rather than theories of value. Even so opinionated a reader of literature as Brooks may finally be of more permanent interest for what his conception of the verbal nature of poetry is than for the judgments that seem to arise from this conception. Of course, he does judge and has held out for the unity of theory and judgment. His first critical book, *Modern Poetry and the Tradition,* makes mighty complaints about Romantic sentimentality, but in *The Well Wrought Urn* he discusses Wordsworth, Keats, and Tennyson in terms that he had previously reserved for the metaphysicals and the moderns.

Few critics have been so outspoken about the matter of evaluation as Northrop Frye. We have already noted his remark that every hierarchy of literary values known to him is based on a "concealed social, moral, or intellectual analogy." [20] This is certainly the case with many critics. The later career of Brooks indicates that even his earlier evaluations may have proceeded from a particular religious stance. Frye's idea of analogy is most obvious among clearly violent critics like Leavis, whose judgments can often be classified, I think, under a social analogy. An interesting study of present-day violent critics would be an attempt to discover the guiding analogy in their judgments. Frye goes on to observe that no criticism that actually provides us with knowledge about literature makes any functional use of judgments of value.[21]

Yet systematic critics have not wanted to go Frye's way with quite his frankness or wholly to divorce evaluation from interpretation. The fundamental impetus of critical theories with which we have been concerned has complicated the problem of value by moving toward contextualism. From this point of view a literary work can no longer be judged by exterior canons. The criticism of Rymer, the excesses of the Neoclassicists, the in-

[20] Northrop Frye, *Anatomy of Criticism* (Princeton, N.J.: Princeton Univ. Press, 1957), p. 23.

[21] Northrop Frye, "Reflections in a Mirror" in Murray Krieger, ed., *Northrop Frye in Modern Criticism* (New York: Columbia Univ. Press, 1966), p. 135.

sistence on the unities or on some quality of style, all prove wanting. Each sets up some kind of "Platonic" form against which the poem is judged. In spite of occasional predilections by recent critics for irony and paradox or other elements of the poem, the theoretical implication of contextualism has been that the poem evolves its own standard of judgment much in the way, perhaps, that Wordsworth claims each poet creates the taste by which he comes to be appreciated. In this view criticism becomes first and foremost a search for the nature of each poem, "nature" meaning in this case the poem's principle of order. Thus Frye announces that criticism "has nothing to do with rejection, only with recognition." [22]

But recognition itself becomes judgment, and the dangers of this are not to be minimized. Too many scholarly journals are too full of essays utterly determined to recognize the existence of a high degree of order and complexity in the most unlikely and, from other vantages, flawed works. Sometimes the reader of such criticism ironically concludes that anything in a work can be justified if only one tries hard enough with enough ingenuity. Alas, it appears that this ingenuity can be learned by almost anyone. There is a temptation occasionally to cry out for a harsh paragraph of Winters or a diatribe by Leavis. Contextual criticism does seem logically unable to do more than recognize and recognize and recognize, unless it deserts its principle of intrinsic order and opts surreptitiously for some critical panacea like sincerity or the presence of a favorite device. Perhaps, after all, the ability of a poem to call for recognition after recognition after recognition is the best sign of its value. That Shakespeare has managed to sustain and survive all the books about his work is proof of something.

In spite of this problem, which may be a genuine dilemma, good criticism is occasionally written, and it is written more often than not when the critic is as aware as he can make himself of the theoretical problems threatening him. Sometimes we sense that he is aware through a combination of intuition, native tact, and good sense; sometimes we recognize that he has earned his insights by long and systematic worrying of the issues. If the critic is sensitive to his job, he becomes aware very quickly of the limitations of his instrument, language. He learns of the irony in his own struggle with words, a struggle, as Joyce Cary remarked, that poets have complained of for well over two thousand years.

[22] Frye, "Letter to the English Institute" in Krieger, *ibid.*, p. 29.

# A SHORT LIST OF BOOKS
# ABOUT CRITICAL THEORY

(Dates are those of first publication)

*Abrams, M. H., *The Mirror and the Lamp: Romantic Theory and the Critical Tradition* (1953)

Atkins, J. W. H., *Literary Criticism in Antiquity*, 2 vols. (1934)

Baldwin, Charles, *Medieval Rhetoric and Poetic* (1928)

*Bate, Walter J., *From Classic to Romantic, Premises of Taste in Eighteenth-Century England* (1946)

*Bosanquet, Bernard, *A History of Aesthetic* (1892)

Bray, René, *La formation de la doctrine classique en France* (1927)

*Butcher, S. L., *Aristotle's Theory of Poetry and Fine Art* (1895)

*Croce, Benedetto, *Aesthetic as Science of Expression and General Linguistic* (1902)

D'Alton, John F., *Roman Literary Theory and Criticism* (1931)

Else, Gerald F., *Aristotle's Poetics: The Argument* (1957)

Erlich, Victor, *Russian Formalism: History–Doctrine* (1955)

Grube, G. M. A., *The Greek and Roman Critics* (1965)

Hathaway, Baxter, *The Age of Criticism, The Late Renaissance in Italy* (1962)

Henn, T. R., *Longinus and English Criticism* (1934)

*Krieger, Murray, *The New Apologists for Poetry* (1956)

*Monk, Samuel H., *The Sublime: A Study of Critical Theories in Eighteenth-Century England* (1933)

Raymond, Marcel, *From Baudelaire to Surrealism* (1933)

Roberts, William Rhys, *Greek Rhetoric and Literary Theory* (1928)

Saintsbury, George, *A History of Criticism and Literary Taste in Europe*, 3 vols. (1900–1904)

*Spingarn, Joel E., *A History of Literary Criticism in the Renaissance* (1898)

Weinberg, Bernard, *A History of Literary Criticism in the Italian Renaissance*, 2 vols. (1961)

* Available in paperback.

Wellek, René, *A History of Modern Criticism,* 4 vols. (1955 ff.)

*Wellek, René, and Warren, Austin, *Theory of Literature* (1949)

*Wimsatt, W. K., and Brooks, Cleanth, *Literary Criticism: A Short History* (1957)

# A SHORT HISTORICAL LIST OF
# IMPORTANT THEORETICAL WORKS

The only hope of a list as short as this is to offer some sense of the development of critical theory. There is obviously not enough room to include all of the major works of critical theory. Except in rare instances I have listed only one work by an author. Works available in English are emphasized throughout.

Plato, *Ion* (*c*. 390 B.C.)

———, *Republic* (*c*. 373 B.C.)

———, *Laws* (*c*. 335 B.C.)

Aristotle, *Poetics* (*c*. 330 B.C.)

Horace, *Art of Poetry* (*Epistle to the Pisos*) (*c*. 25 B.C.)

Longinus, *On the Sublime* (*c*. 80 A.D.)

St. Thomas Aquinas, *Summa Theologica* (*c*. 1265)

Dante Alighieri, Letter to Can Grande della Scala (*c*. 1318)

Giovanni Boccaccio, *Life of Dante* (1364)

———, The Fourteenth Book of *The Genealogy of the Gentile Gods* (*c*. 1365)

Giangiorgio Trissino, *Poetics* (1529, 1563)

Joachim Du Bellay, *The Defense and Illustration of the French Language* (1549)

Giraldi Cinthio, *On the Composition of Romances, Comedies, Tragedies, etc.* (1554)

Julius Caesar Scaliger, *Poetics* (1561)

Antonio Minturno, *The Art of Poetry* (1564)

Pierre de Ronsard, *A Brief on the Art of French Poetry* (1565)

Ludovico Castelvetro, *The Poetics of Aristotle Translated and Annotated* (1571)

Francesco Patrizzi, *Poetics* (1586)

Jacopo Mazzoni, *On the Defense of the Comedy of Dante* (1587)

George Puttenham, *The Arte of English Poesie* (1589)

Torquato Tasso, *Discourses on the Heroic Poem* (1594)

Philip Sidney, *An Apologie for Poesie* (1595)

Samuel Daniel, *A Defense of Ryme* (*c*. 1602)

Francis Bacon, *The Advancement of Learning* (1605)

Ben Jonson, *Timber; or Discoveries* (*c.* 1620–25)

Thomas Hobbes, Answer to Davenant's Preface to *Gondibert* (1650)

Pierre Corneille, *Discourses* (1660)

John Dryden, *An Essay of Dramatic Poetry* (1668)

Nicholas Boileau-Dupréaux, *The Art of Poetry* (1680)

Alexander Pope, *Essay on Criticism* (1711)

Joseph Addison, "On the Pleasures of the Imagination" (1712)

Giambattista Vico, *The New Science* (1725)

Voltaire, *Essay on Epic Poetry* (1727)

Alexander Baumgarten, *Aesthetics* (1750)

Louis Le Clerq, Comte de Buffon, *Discourse on Style* (1753)

Edmund Burke, *A Philosophical Inquiry into the Origin of Our Ideas of the Sublime and Beautiful* (1757)

David Hume, "Of the Standard of Taste" (1757)

Samuel Johnson, *Rasselas,* Chapter X (1759)

Edward Young, "Conjectures on Original Composition" (1759)

Richard Hurd, *Letters on Chivalry and Romance* (1762)

Gotthold Ephraim Lessing, *Laocöon* (1766)

Joshua Reynolds, *Discourses on Art* (1769–90)

Samuel Johnson, *Lives of the English Poets* (1779–81)

Immanuel Kant, *Critique of Judgment* (1790)

Johann Friedrich von Schiller, *Letters on the Aesthetic Education of Man* (1793–95)

William Wordsworth, Preface to the Second Edition of *Lyrical Ballads* (1800)

Friedrich Wilhelm Joseph von Schelling, "On the Relation of the Plastic Arts to Nature" (1807)

William Blake, Annotations to Reynolds' *Discourses* (1808)

August Wilhelm von Schlegel, *Lectures on Dramatic Art and Literature* (1808)

Friedrich von Schlegel, *Lectures on the History of Literature* (1815)

Samuel Taylor Coleridge, *Biographia Literaria* (1817)

John Keats, Letters written in 1817–18

William Hazlitt, "On Poetry in General" (1818)

Thomas Love Peacock, "The Four Ages of Poetry" (1820)

Percy Bysshe Shelley, *A Defence of Poetry* (1821)

Johann Wolfgang von Goethe, *Conversations with Eckermann* (1822–32)

John Stuart Mill, "What Is Poetry?" (1833)

Vissarion Belinski, *On the General Significance of the Term Literature* (1834–40)

Théophile Gautier, Preface to *Mademoiselle de Maupin* (1835)

John Ruskin, "Of the Pathetic Fallacy" (1840)

Charles Augustin Saint-Beuve, "What Is a Classic?" (1850)

Edgar Allan Poe, "The Poetic Principle" (1850)

Charles Baudelaire, "The Queen of the Faculties" (1859)

Hippolyte Taine, *History of English Literature* (1864)

Emile Zola, *The Experimental Novel* (1880)

Friedrich Nietzsche, *The Birth of Tragedy from the Spirit of Music* (1872)

Walter Pater, *Studies in the History of the Renaissance* (1873)

Matthew Arnold, "The Study of Poetry" (1880)

Oscar Wilde, "The Decay of Lying" (1889)

William Dean Howells, *Criticism and Fiction* (1891)

Stéphane Mallarmé, "Mystery in Literature" (1895)

Leo Nikolaivich Tolstoy, *What Is Art?* (1895)

William Butler Yeats, "The Symbolism of Poetry" (1900)

Henri Bergson, *Laughter* (1901)

A. C. Bradley, "Poetry for Poetry's Sake" (1901)

Benedetto Croce, *Aesthetic* (1902)

Sigmund Freud, "Creative Writers and Daydreaming" (1908)

Edward Bullough, " 'Psychical Distance' as a Factor in Art and an Aesthetic Principle" (1912)

Roger Frye, *Vision and Design* (1920)

T. E. Hulme, *Speculations* (1924)

Virginia Woolf, "Mr. Bennett and Mrs. Brown" (1924)

Owen Barfield, *Poetic Diction* (1928)

I. A. Richards, *Principles of Literary Criticism* (1928)

William Empson, *Seven Types of Ambiguity* (1930)

Giovanni Gentile, *The Philosophy of Art* (1931)

F. R. Leavis, *New Bearings in English Poetry* (1932)

T. S. Eliot, *Selected Essays 1917–1932* (1932)

Carl G. Jung, *Modern Man in Search of a Soul* (1933)

Maud Bodkin, *Archetypal Patterns in Poetry* (1934)

D. G. James, *Scepticism and Poetry* (1937)

George Lukacs, *The Historical Novel* (1937)

John Crowe Ransom, *The World's Body* (1938)

R. G. Collingwood, *The Principles of Art* (1938)

Cleanth Brooks, Jr., *Modern Poetry and the Tradition* (1939)

W. M. Urban, *Language and Reality* (1939)

Kenneth Burke, *The Philosophy of Literary Form* (1941)

Susanne K. Langer, *Philosophy in a New Key* (1942)

Ernst Cassirer, *An Essay on Man* (1944)

Erich Auerbach, *Mimesis* (1946)

Allen Tate, *On the Limits of Poetry* (1948)

Francis Fergusson, *The Idea of a Theater* (1949)

Jean-Paul Sartre, *What Is Literature?* (1950)

R. S. Crane (ed.) *Critics and Criticism* (1952)

R. S. Crane, *The Languages of Criticism and the Structure of Poetry* (1953)

Jacques Maritain, *Creative Intuition in Art and Poetry* (1953)

W. K. Wimsatt, *The Verbal Icon* (1954)

Philip Wheelwright, *The Burning Fountain* (1954)

Eliseo Vivas, *Creation and Discovery* (1955)

R. P. Blackmur, *The Lion and the Honeycomb* (1955)

Georges Poulet, *Studies in Human Time* (1956)

Northrop Frye, *Anatomy of Criticism* (1957)

E. H. Gombrich, *Art and Illusion* (1960)

Wayne Booth, *The Rhetoric of Fiction* (1961)

Murray Krieger, *The Play and Place of Criticism* (1967)

E. D. Hirsch, Jr., *Validity in Interpretation* (1967)